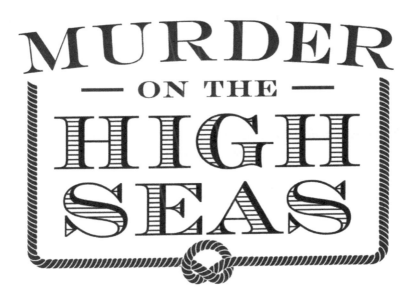

MURDER
ON THE
HIGH SEAS

MARTIN BAGGOLEY

FONTHILL

This book is dedicated to Albert Snr, Harriet, Chrissie, Lilly, Elsie, Albert Jnr, Hilda and Joan.

Fonthill Media Limited
Fonthill Media LLC
www.fonthillmedia.com
office@fonthillmedia.com

First published in the United Kingdom and the United States of America
2014

ISBN 978 1 78155 118 9

Typeset in 10.5 pt on 13.5 pt Sabon Lt Std
Printed and bound by CPI Group (UK) Ltd, Croydon, CR0 4YY

Contents

1

The *Adventurer*, 1812

For those prepared to take the risks involved, there were fortunes to be made in whale oil and Captain James Keith was one such man. He invested his life savings of £2,000 in the purchase of a whaling ship named the *Adventurer* and in September 1811, she sailed out of Portsmouth harbour bound for the South Seas. This proved to be an ill-fated voyage and as nothing was heard of the ship and her crew for many months, she was presumed lost. That was until mid-1812 when Charles Palm, the Swedish second mate, cooper Samuel Telling, a seaman named William Wright and Henry Mendis, a boy deckhand, arrived on foot at Cape Lopez, a Portuguese settlement on the African coast. Palm acted as the group's spokesman and he advised the authorities they were the only surviving members of the *Adventurer*'s crew and recounted a story of great hardship and tragedy.

For the first six months of the voyage, all was said to have gone well. However, first of all, the elderly first mate, William Smith, fell ill and died of natural causes and later, Captain Keith was killed in a tragic accident. Keith was said to have harpooned a whale but in doing so, the line became entangled with his legs, dragging him into the ocean and he drowned before he could be rescued. Furthermore, two African hands, who were known as Joe and John and who were signed on by the skipper when supplies were being taken on board, appeared to panic following his death and jumped overboard, despite the vessel being 50 miles from land.

There were now eleven members of the crew remaining, but no one was capable of navigating the ship and it was therefore decided to abandon her. Provisions were loaded into her two small boats, in which the crew, six in one and five in the other, spent three days. Unfortunately, one of the boats was hit by a large wave and a boy was lost overboard. Eventually, the boats reached land and on the first night the survivors slept on the beach. The following day they were attacked by local tribesmen who stripped them naked and were forced to march through the jungle for many weeks as they were destined to be sold as white slaves. The trek was horrific and six of the crew died of disease, fatigue or cruelty at the hands of their captors. However, when they were handed over to a leading slave dealer close to Cape Lopez, he chose to release them, perhaps fearing reprisals from the British in particular if it was ever discovered he had sold a number of their countrymen into slavery.

There were no reasons for the Portuguese to detain the four survivors, who were allowed to return to Europe. Palm and Wright joined the crew of the *Dart,* a British schooner, which was not due to return home for several months. Telling and Mendis were taken on board a Portuguese ship, which was sailing to Liverpool, where on arrival Telling was in such poor health that he was taken immediately to a nearby hospital for urgent treatment. Mendis wrote to his mother in London to advise her of his safe return and to ask her to send him enough money with which to pay his coach fare home. In the meantime, a kindly old mariner, who took pity on the boy, allowed him to lodge with him and his wife until the money arrived.

Mendis visited Telling daily and after a week was astonished to find Palm and Wright also in the hospital recovering from their ordeal. It emerged that the captain of the *Dart* had decided to sail to Liverpool rather than prolong the voyage as he had planned originally. In Liverpool, the *Adventurer*'s four survivors had given similar accounts to that which Palm told the Portuguese authorities at Cape Lopez and it was agreed by port officials that they would be allowed to leave when they regained their health. Mendis was the first to leave Liverpool after the money arrived from his mother, which enabled him to pay his fare home.

It was now early November and once in the safety of his family home and out of the reach of the others, Mendis had a different tale to tell. He made a statement before Shadwell magistrates in which he confirmed that the account of their capture by local tribesmen and the ordeal that followed until reaching Cape Lopez was correct; however, he now claimed that the truth of what occurred on the *Adventurer* had not been told. Having listened to this revised version of events, the magistrates ordered three Bow Street runners, Glennen, Wortley and Goff, to travel to Liverpool and arrest Wright, Palm and Telling. By the time they arrived, Wright had left the hospital and was never traced, but Palm and Telling were brought back to London in chains to face justice for the crimes for which Mendis alleged they were responsible.

The youngster was unable to give the date on which the events he now described took place, other than to say they occurred about six months into the voyage. He began by saying that it was night-time and Palm was on watch. Mendis was asleep in his bunk in the same cabin as the captain and first mate when they were suddenly woken by George Rowe, a seaman who was at the helm and who shouted to the skipper, 'Captain Keith, there is something wrong on deck.' Wearing only his nightshirt, the captain rushed up the steps and screamed, 'Turn out, turn out.' The first mate ran out of the cabin and a few moments later Mendis heard him shout, 'Oh Lord.' Mendis followed and realised that all the crew had assembled on deck. He was horrified to see Palm and two other Swedish crewmembers tossing the body of the captain over the ship's side. It was then he became aware of the first mate, in a pleading voice, shouting from the sea, 'Boat, boat!' However, there was no attempt to rescue him and he quickly fell silent.

Palm forced each member of the crew to swear an oath on the Bible that he might never see the light of Heaven if he divulged anything of what had taken place that night. Afterwards, the captain's belongings were searched and his money and valuables shared out equally among the crew. Mendis admitted to the magistrates that he took the oath and was handed a share of the captain's money, but did so only to avoid being killed by the others. As soon as he was at home with his mother and felt safe, he had told the truth. Nevertheless, it is unlikely that he intended to implicate Telling as he was on friendly terms with him. Indeed, when questioned by the magistrates following his arrest, Telling not only corroborated much of what the youngster had said, but was able to provide more detailed information about what he witnessed on the *Adventurer* on the night in question. He claimed to have watched the captain step out of his cabin and heard him shout to Palm, 'Charles, what are you about?' However, the Swede did not reply but hit the captain several blows to the head with a cooper's hammer. As he fell, the captain cried out, 'Oh Charles, you have done for me.' It was at this moment that the first mate came on deck, whereupon another Swedish crewmember, who was obviously in cahoots with Palm, struck him a number of times with a cook's axe, forcing him to stagger and fall. Telling then watched as Palm and the other Swede threw the two men into the sea. Although the captain was dead, Telling had heard the mate begging for mercy from the water but as Mendis had already explained, his pleas were ignored.

It was then that Palm insisted the oath should be sworn and Telling was adamant that he agreed to do so, only to ensure he was not murdered by Palm and his co-conspirators. The two black seamen, who had taken no part in the crimes and who were clearly terrified, were each handed a tot of rum, apparently in a gesture meant to reassure them. Yet as they drank, both were shot by another of the Swedes and their bodies thrown into the sea. One had survived the shooting and was clinging to the ship's rudder. Palm took hold of a spade and began to hit the man's hands, which he threatened to cut off if he did not let go, thus forcing him to loosen his grip and he too disappeared beneath the waves. He acknowledged that he helped throw the two black sailors over the ship's side, but only because Palm demanded he did so. He insisted he played no part in planning the murders. Nevertheless, he was charged together with Palm as the crown felt that unlike Mendis, he had not given a true account when the opportunity arose for him to do so after arriving in Liverpool.

When first interrogated, Palm had denied taking part in any criminal activity on board the *Adventurer*. He claimed to have been aware of some disquiet among the crew after Captain Keith had put them on short rations within days of leaving England, but the only minor argument he claimed to have had with Keith was over his wages. He continued to maintain that he knew nothing other than what he had been told by his shipmates and that the captain was dragged into the sea after harpooning a whale following Smith's death from natural causes. As for the African hands, he claimed they jumped overboard of their own volition following the captain's death and Palm surmised they must have feared they would not be taken home and believing the vessel was close to land, decided to try and swim to the coast.

The trial of Palm and Telling took place in the Court of Admiralty in mid-December and they were only charged with the murder of Captain Keith. Palm was offered the option of having his countrymen comprise half the jury, but he replied that he preferred to place his fate in the hands of Englishmen rather than have a single Swede sitting in judgement of him. Telling's defence was based on his initial statement made in Liverpool, to have been coerced into participating, but Palm had decided to change his story. He acknowledged that he witnessed the murders of the captain and first mate, but stated he took no part in planning or carrying out the killings. Telling and the other Swedes, now dead, were the ringleaders and they had forced him to throw the captain's body into the sea.

The jury took just fifteen minutes to find the defendants guilty of murder. The death sentence was passed on both men and the recriminations began immediately. Telling turned to face Palm in the dock and shouted, 'I owe this sentence to you. Did you not tell me if I did not join you I would be killed?' Palm denied the accusation and they could be heard arguing as they were led out of the dock. There was little sympathy for Palm but many believed Telling had been treated harshly by the court, but there would be no reprieve.

For centuries, those convicted of piracy and murders on the high seas were tried at the Court of Admiralty in London and if convicted and sentenced to death, they were hanged at Execution Dock in Wapping. The scaffold was sited a little beyond the low-tide mark to symbolise where the authority of the Admiralty began. In common with all executions at the time, they were carried out in public, were highly ritualised and were intended to act as a deterrent to others.

On the morning of 21 December 1812, Palm and Telling, who had spent the night in Marshalsea Prison, were placed in an open cart that formed part of a much longer procession. At its head was the High Court Marshal on horseback and in his hand he carried a silver oar, which represented the Admiralty's authority. The solemn procession made its way over London Bridge, passed the Tower of London and along streets lined with many thousands of onlookers. The cart came to a halt outside the Turks Head Inn at which they were allowed a last drink of ale. Throughout the journey, Palm, who was aged about fifty years old, put on a brave face, apparently unconcerned at his fate. He was chewing a quid of tobacco and offered a piece to the twenty-five-year-old Telling who declined the offer.

By far the most unpleasant feature of the executions at Wapping was the hangman's use of a short rope, which ensured the condemned men suffered a prolonged death by strangulation. The crowd witnessed their desperate struggles, which lasted for many minutes and were known as the 'Marshal's Dance'. The bodies remained hanging for all to see for three tides before being cut down and sent for dissection.

The last ever hanging at Execution Dock took place in 1830 after which those convicted of capital crimes committed at sea and who were tried in London were executed at Newgate.

2

HMS *Griffon*, 1812

On the morning of 27 October 1812, a court martial, presided over by Vice Admiral Thomas Foley, was held aboard HMS *Monmouth,* at anchor in the Downs, an area of sea off the Kent coast. Standing in the dock and facing a charge of wilful murder was twenty-seven-year-old Lieutenant Richard Stewart Gamage RN. Those who knew him were astounded that he should find himself in this position. He was born in Walthamstow and his father was a long-serving captain of an Indiaman with the East India Company. His son was clearly destined for a career at sea and the young Gamage entered the Royal Navy in 1801. He saw a great deal of active service and distinguished himself in a number of sea battles. His reputation was enhanced further when he jumped into the sea in the dead of night, a highly dangerous and courageous act, to rescue a marine who had fallen overboard. Gamage was promoted to the rank of lieutenant in 1808 and following his return from a voyage to China, he joined HMS *Griffon* as first lieutenant in June 1812.

His alleged victim was Sergeant of Marines Lake and the crime was said to have occurred on the *Griffon,* a sixteen-gun brig-sloop, which had been captured from the French and renamed in 1808. On the day Lake died, the ship was anchored in the Downs and her commander, Captain Trollope, had gone ashore, leaving Gamage in temporary charge. The tragedy began to unfold when Lake was disrespectful to the ship's carpenter, who was his senior officer. The carpenter approached Gamage to make a formal report of Lake's behaviour. Gamage decided that Captain Trollope need not be troubled and that a minor summary punishment was appropriate, leading him to order Lake to march up and down the quarterdeck a number of times while carrying his musket. However, the sergeant refused to obey the order and his insolent manner so enraged Gamage that he rushed to his cabin and returned carrying his sabre, which was still in its scabbard. The lieutenant repeated the order, which Lake once again refused to obey as a result of which, Gamage withdrew the sabre and with it he tapped Lake's musket several times. This appeared to result in the sergeant finally deciding to carry out the order as he shouldered arms and the lieutenant's weapon was returned to its scabbard. Nevertheless, rather than march along the quarterdeck as ordered, Lake threw the musket down and with an obscene oath made it clear he had no intention of obeying the lieutenant. This act of insubordination was a step too far for Gamage who withdrew his sabre and plunged it into Lake's chest, killing him instantly.

In his defence, the accused officer relied heavily on a lengthy personal statement he read to the members of the tribunal. He began by acknowledging the truth of much of what was said about the incident and attempted to explain why he behaved as he did. Gamage expressed what was recognised as his genuine remorse for what happened, but added that he was deeply shocked when accused of murder. He insisted that the stabbing of the sergeant was unpremeditated and was carried out in the face of extreme provocation as the deceased had refused to obey a lawful order. It was ironic, Gamage suggested, as the task he gave Lake to perform was one of the very least he could have imposed in order to avoid a more serious penalty being given later by the captain on his return to the ship. He claimed to have drawn his sabre, not with the intention of endangering Lake's life, but simply to enforce obedience. Gamage reminded the tribunal that he had returned the weapon to its scabbard when it seemed that Lake was about to obey the order and it was only produced again in response to what the lieutenant described as 'The imposing attitude of the man, the fierce arrangement of his features and his high ingratitude and disdain.'

A number of senior officers spoke of the lieutenant's excellent character and outstanding service record. Also, a testimonial in his support, which had been signed by the entire crew of the *Griffon*, was handed to Vice Admiral Foley. Having considered their verdict with great care, the tribunal members returned with a guilty verdict of wilful murder and Gamage was sentenced to death. However, in view of his service history and previous good character, he was advised that a strong recommendation for mercy would be forwarded to the Admiralty by the members of the Tribunal. The condemned lieutenant's fate was the subject of lengthy discussions involving the nation's most senior law officers and the Admiralty, and it was also raised at cabinet level. Nevertheless, Gamage appeared to accept as soon as the death sentence was passed on him that there would be no reprieve. He immediately began to refuse food intending to starve himself to death and thereby avoid the ignominy of a public hanging. His instincts proved to be correct and after almost a month's deliberations it was learnt that he would be executed on the morning of 23 November on board HMS *Griffon*. Those close to him believed that his health had deteriorated so much since the court martial, that had there been any more delay he would have achieved his wish to beat the noose by dying of starvation.

On the eve of his execution, Gamage was visited by many of the ship's distressed crew, several of whom asked for a lock of his hair to remember him by. He fell asleep at one o'clock in the morning, but had finished a letter to his sister Eliza in which he wrote, 'Yes, indeed, the *Griffon* is now sad and silent. Always pray for the safety of the men who loved me as they do.' He rose at six o'clock and dressed himself in black and spent the next three hours in prayer.

Two days before the execution was to take place, a general memorandum was sent to all of the Royal Navy vessels at anchor in the Downs. It directed that on the morning of 23 November, two small boats from each ship were to row to the *Griffon* and assemble alongside. At nine o'clock, a gun would be fired and a yellow flag hoisted aboard the *Griffon* to indicate that the punishment was to be carried out. All work was to cease on the other ships and their crews were to line up on the decks and climb the rigging in order that every man should witness the hanging. Work was not to resume until the body was cut down and during this time, sections of the 19th and 28th Articles of War, which related to discipline on a warship, were to be read out by the officers. The memorandum was accompanied by the following personal dispatch from Vice Admiral Foley in which he expressed the hope that witnessing the event would serve as a deterrent to others:

The Commander-in-Chief most earnestly desires to direct the particular attention of the Fleet to the melancholy scene they are now called to attend – a scene which offers a strong and much he hopes, an impressive lesson to every person in it – a lesson to all who are in command and to all who are to obey. Lieutenant Gamage is represented by every person who knew him and by the unanimous voice of the *Griffon* ship's company, as a humane, compassionate man, a kind indulgent officer; yet for want of that guard which every man should keep over his passions, this kind, humane, compassionate man, commits the dreadful crime of murder! Let his example strike deep into the minds of all who witness his unhappy end and whatever their general disposition may be, let them learn from him, that if they are not always watchful to retrain their passions within their proper bounds, one moment of intemperate anger may destroy the hopes of a well spent, honourable life and bring them to an untimely and disgraceful death. And let those who are to obey, learn from the conduct of the Sergeant, the fatal effects which may result from contempt and insolent conduct towards their superiors. By repeated insolence, the Sergeant overcame the gentle disposition of Lieutenant Gamage and by irritating and inflaming his passion, occasioned his own death. The Commander-in-Chief hopes that this afflicting lesson may not be offered in vain, but seriously contemplating the awful example before them, every officer and every man will learn from it, never to suffer himself to be driven by ill-governed passion to treat with cruelty or violence those over whom he is to command, nor by disobedience or disrespect to rouse the passions of those whom it is his duty to obey and respect.

At nine-thirty, although much weakened, Gamage walked purposefully from his cabin, preceded by a clergyman. A fellow officer was at each side to provide support and the other officers of the *Griffon,* all of whom were in tears, followed behind. On reaching the platform, Gamage bowed to his shipmates a number of times and thanked them for the efforts they had made to try and save him. At ten o'clock, the yardarm halter was placed around his neck and he was hauled up; he reportedly died without a struggle. Four hours later, Gamage's body was taken ashore and in the presence of Captain Trollope and most of the *Griffon*'s crew, he was buried in the grounds of the Royal Naval Hospital in Deal.

3

The *Jane*, 1821

It was mid-May in 1821 and the schooner *Jane* was in the harbour at Gibraltar, taking on a cargo of raisins, oil, bees wax, silk, aniseed and paper in readiness for her forthcoming voyage to Brazil. In addition, eight barrels containing 38,180 silver Spanish dollars were taken on board. Thomas Johnston was the master and there were two serving crewmembers: James Paterson, an experienced seaman, and Andrew Camelier, a nineteen year old from Malta. In the week before setting sail, five seamen were recruited and these were Peter Smith and David Robertson Strachan, both nineteen years of age, twenty-five-year-old Indian, Johanna Dhura, twenty-four-year-old Frenchman Francois Gautiez was taken on as cook and Peter Haemen, who was thirty-six years old, was to act as mate.

The *Jane* set sail on 19 May and it was only a few days into the voyage when Haemen approached Strachan, Smith and Paterson with a startling proposal. He informed them that he planned to murder the captain, take command of the boat and steal the coins. Haemen assured them that they would not have to become involved in the killing as he would commit the act alone. He could navigate the ship but he would need a crew and for their help, each man would receive an equal share of the silver dollars. The three others dismissed his suggestion out of hand and having heard no more such talk over the following days, they presumed if he had been serious that he had abandoned the idea. However, they were wrong for Haemen had persuaded Gautiez to join him.

On the evening of 6 June, Captain Johnston was on watch with Strachan and Dhura. At midnight, they were relieved by Paterson, Haemen and Gautiez. The Frenchman was standing in for Smith who had injured his leg a few days earlier. The captain retired to his bunk in his cabin, which was situated next to that in which Camelier was sleeping. In the early hours of 7 June, the youngster awoke to the sound of what he immediately recognised to be that of a musket shot in the captain's cabin. He rushed out on to the deck and was shocked to see Haemen beating Paterson violently about the head with the butt of a musket, eventually forcing him to the deck and unable to defend himself he soon fell silent and no longer moved. The captain emerged from his cabin, holding his head from which blood was flowing out of a wound. He was followed by the Frenchman who was also holding a musket, with which he had shot the skipper. Nevertheless, he had failed to kill him and the confused and stunned Captain Johnston cried out, 'What is this? What is this?' He received no reply for he was struck violently from behind by Gautiez and fell unconscious to the deck.

Strachan and Dhura who were asleep in the forecastle were now awake and they opened the hatch. Before they were able to step out, Haemen, who was wielding an axe, ran towards them screaming, 'Don't come up!' They retreated and the mate locked the hatch behind them. Sometime later, Camelier and Dhura were ordered to come on deck, but Smith and Strachan remained locked up. Haemen and Gautiez explained that they did not feel they could trust Smith and Strachan as they believed they had warned the captain of their plans to take over the boat. They continued by saying they were going to take the *Jane* into Scottish waters where it was intended to sink her and make off with the dollars. Camelier and Dhura were terrified and the Indian pleaded with the mate and cook by stating, 'Don't kill me, I will help you.' He was told that if he and the Maltese youngster helped, they would receive an equal share of the coins and when ordered to assist in throwing the bodies overboard, Dhura readily agreed. As he did so, he noticed that although Paterson was obviously dead, the skipper was still breathing as he was thrown into the sea.

It soon became evident that Smith and Strachan were to be murdered also. The mate nailed their cabin door shut and bored two holes in the adjoining wall of the cabin next door. Gaps in the timbers were sealed with a paste mixture of flour and water and a fire was lit in the adjoining cabin. It was intended that the smoke would be channelled through the two holes and into the cabin occupied by the two men so they would suffocate. Twenty-four hours later, Haemen opened up the forecastle, expecting to find two bodies but incredibly, the men had survived as the cabin had not been made completely airtight. Nevertheless, they were in great distress and the door was again nailed shut. On the third day, the door was opened and both men were still alive. They were ordered on deck and fearing they were about to be murdered, Dhura begged Haemen and Gautiez not to kill them. After a brief discussion, they agreed but insisted that the men swear the following oath on the Bible: 'May God Almighty never save my soul if I ever reveal what has passed.' Afterwards, the men were promised their lives would be spared if they followed orders and for the remainder of the voyage were forced to sleep on the deck so their captors could keep watch on them.

The *Lark,* which was sailing out of New York, was passed at sea and when hailed by her captain, Haemen replied they were thirteen days out of Archangel. Otherwise, the voyage towards Scotland was uneventful and the *Jane* eventually anchored off the Isle of Barra. Her lifeboat was unsuitable for their planned escape from the area and Haemen and Gautiez ordered Strachan and Smith to go ashore and purchase a larger boat, in which the six men could leave after scuttling the *Jane.* Afterwards, it was intended to report the vessel and the two murdered men to have been lost at sea. Sixty silver dollars were paid for a small fishing boat and the *Jane* sailed towards the Isle of Lewis, which was reached on 23 July. Some hours later, Camelier and Smith were ordered below deck to open the seacocks and bore holes in the hull, thereby ensuring the *Jane* sank. The six men reached shore where some of the coins were shared out and many more were buried to be retrieved later. However, the location chosen to scuttle the *Jane* was not as deserted as they believed it to be. An islander saw the vessel lying on her side before she disappeared beneath the waves.

As the weather was poor and there were high winds, the islander believed she had been blown against the rocks and sank. He reported what he had seen to Mr McIver, the area's Surveyor of Customs, who suspected the ship might have been carrying contraband goods. He and a number of his officers went to investigate and they found the six men and the fishing boat on the shore. McIver questioned Haemen who introduced himself as Captain George Sadwell of the supposedly doomed vessel, which he claimed had been sailing from New York to Liverpool. A brief search was made, which revealed nothing suspicious as the men were found to possess only a few of the silver dollars. McIver and his men took their leave and it was not until a few minutes later that Haemen noticed Camelier was missing.

The youngster had followed McIver and as soon as he caught up with him, he told of the murders, the seizure of the ship, its sinking and of the buried dollars. The customs man took Camelier with him and left two of his officers to keep watch on the five remaining seamen until he could return with several armed colleagues. He did so later that same day and led a raid on the little camp. A search was made and in excess of 30,000 silver coins were discovered concealed in the men's clothing and buried in the ground nearby. All were taken into custody and as the *Jane* was scuttled in Scottish waters, it was decided that the alleged crimes came under Scottish jurisdiction. It was accepted by the crown that Camelier, Dhura, Smith and Strachan had acted under duress and as they agreed to testify for the prosecution, no charges were laid against them.

The trial of Haemen and Gautiez opened on 26 November at the High Court of Admiralty in Edinburgh before Sir John Connell, Judge Admiral of Scotland. They were charged with the murders of Johnston and Paterson, the attempted murder of Smith and Strachan by suffocation, the unlawful sinking of the *Jane* and the seizure of her cargo. The four former crewmembers were important witnesses and their evidence formed the basis of the crown's case. Nevertheless, the accused had destroyed all of Captain Johnston's documents, so it was necessary to prove that they were not entitled to the silver dollars. Therefore, another significant witness was Abraham Levy Bensusan, a London insurance agent who made the trip north to provide details of the ownership of the coins, the other cargo and the boat.

The prisoners had claimed initially that Captain Johnston murdered Paterson following a dispute and feeling threatened, the six remaining crewmembers were forced to kill him in self-defence. As the trial progressed, their barrister attempted to persuade the jury that as the four shipmates and main accusers had participated in the events on board the *Jane,* it would be folly to send the prisoners to the gallows on the evidence provided by such men. It was therefore suggested that the most appropriate verdict would be 'not proven'. However, the jury was not convinced and reached unanimous guilty verdicts to all the charges in respect of both defendants. In his concluding remarks to the now condemned men, Sir John Connell told them:

> You landed on the shore of these islands, a land where the innocent are always sure of an asylum but the guilty of detection. If there were a punishment severer than death you deserve it. But the object of our laws is example not vindictive revenge. Sentence of death must now pass upon you and in every human probability it will be carried into execution. The door of mercy is open to the penitent offender of the laws, but to the murderer and pirate it must be ever shut.

He directed that they be taken to Calton Prison where they were to be fed only on bread and water until 9 January 1822 when they were to be hanged and afterwards their bodies dissected. Those convicted in Scotland of piracy and other capital crimes committed at sea were hanged within the high water mark on Leith Sands. No execution had taken place there for almost forty years, when, in February 1782, Captain Potts of the privateer *Dreadnought* met his end on the Sands for plundering the *White Swan*. It was therefore inevitable, given their rarity, that there was a massive amount of public interest in the hangings of Haemen and Gautiez. This was especially so as it was realised that these might be the last to take place on the Sands, which indeed they proved to be. Executions were traditionally highly ritualised spectacles intended to deter others from crime and to demonstrate the supremacy of the state and its institutions, and the hangings of Haemen and Gautiez, for which a temporary gallows was erected, would be no exception.

At a little after eight o'clock, the local magistrates and their attendants walked slowly from the council chambers to the prison where a detachment of the 3rd Dragoon Guards was standing guard. The dignitaries were taken to the condemned cell in which the prisoners and their spiritual advisers were waiting. Reverend Wallace was comforting Gautiez, a Catholic, and Reverend Dr John Campbell of the Church of Scotland was with Haemen.

At nine-thirty, the prison gates were thrown open and three carriages emerged, carrying a number of council officers and prison officials, including the chaplain, Mr Porteous. Following in a cart were the condemned men and accompanying the vehicles on foot were a large number of local police officers and a detachment of cavalry. The procession crossed Regent Bridge, travelled along Leith Street, Leith Walk and Constitution Street as it made its way to the shore and as it did so, the bell of South Leith Church rang out. Gautiez was downcast but Haemen was smiling as he waved enthusiastically to the many thousands of spectators who lined the route to the execution site. He had explained earlier to a prison warder that he would be doing so and it was his way of thanking the people of Edinburgh and Leith for the great kindness they had shown to his wife and children. As soon as she had heard of her husband's arrest, Mrs Haemen, a French woman he had met when a prisoner of war in France, had immediately left the family home in Sunderland with their four children and made her way to Edinburgh to be close to him. She was destitute but the people of the district learnt of her plight and collected a large amount of money, enabling her to find suitable accommodation during her stay and to pay for her sad journey home. This included three guineas, collected by members of the jury at her husband's trial.

The two men climbed the steps of the scaffold and Gautiez knelt in private and silent prayer. Haemen joined Dr Campbell in reading the 51st Psalm and afterwards stepped forward to address the crowd assembled on the shore, to acknowledge the justness of their punishment. He and Gautiez shook hands with the magistrates and churchmen and finally with each other. At eleven-twenty, Haemen gave an agreed signal to the executioner that they were ready and his last words were, 'Lord Jesus receive my soul.' The bodies were left to hang for forty minutes before they were cut down and taken to Dr Alexander Munro, Professor of Anatomy at Edinburgh University, for dissection.

4

The *Amelia*, 1834

On 24 August 1834, the brig *Mars* was 500 miles into her voyage from Fernando Po to her home port of Liverpool when a member of the watch noticed a small boat with a makeshift sail in which there appeared to be two men. Captain Henry Irving altered course to investigate, believing the occupants to be in difficulty. However, as he drew near, the men in the boat jumped into the water and made a futile attempt to swim away. They were taken on board the *Mars* and were clearly fortunate to have been spotted as they had only a little beef and no water and could not have survived for much longer. They were black Africans who gave their anglicised names: Jumbo and Bottle of Beer.

The rescued men spoke little English but were able to explain that they had been taken on as boat-boys on the *Amelia,* a brig under the command of Captain Benjamin Glasscock, which traded in ivory and gold dust along the coast of West Africa. They had decided to jump ship, despite the great distance from land, as they claimed they had been deprived of food. Also, the captain threatened to sell them into slavery or take them to England rather than return them to their homes when their duties on the *Amelia* were completed as he had promised when they joined his crew.

They had no choice other than to sail to Liverpool on the *Mars* and on arrival they were lodged in the local workhouse to await a ship on which they could work their passage home. Yet before they could do so, Jumbo and Bottle of Beer were arrested and charged with the murder of Captain Glasscock and wounding William Stubbs, a seaman on the *Amelia*. Stubbs was one of several members of the ship's crew who arrived back in England shortly after the Africans and on learning they were in the port, called for their arrests. Jumbo and Bottle of Beer duly appeared before Liverpool's mayor, Alderman Wright.

Two other seamen, Henry Dobie and John Gould, who had been members of the *Amelia*'s crew, also spoke against them. Stubbs and Dobie had dreadful and recently inflicted facial wounds, which they claimed were caused by the accused aboard the ship in the early hours of 20 August 1834. They were also said to have murdered the captain, ship's steward and carpenter before setting fire to the vessel. Stubbs had lost his left ear, there was a large scar on his left cheek and part of his neck had been hacked away. A deep scar extended across Dobie's face from his cheekbone to his mouth and his nose was horribly disfigured. Having listened to the statements of the three seamen, Alderman Wright directed that the two prisoners be taken to London to appear at the Old Bailey in the Admiralty Court where their trial took place on 6 March 1835.

Stubbs was the first witness to be called by the crown and he began by telling the court he had been away from England since November 1830 when he was taken on as a seaman on the *Calypso* on which he remained for two years before joining HMS *Pelorus*. He subsequently left the Royal Navy after learning he had inherited some property and a large amount of money. Stubbs was taken on as a crewmember of the *Amelia* when she was in Cameroon for the return journey to England. The crew comprised the captain, the witness, two other seamen, William Rourke and Henry Dobie, William Griffiths, a cooper, the cook was John Royal, the steward who was known as Campigny, and John Gould who was the ship's mate. A carpenter, whose name was not known, went missing at the same time as the captain and was presumed to be dead, but there was no direct evidence being presented that the two accused were responsible for his death. Stubbs next described what he claimed to have witnessed in the early hours of 20 August 1834 when the *Amelia* was 300 miles from the coast of West Africa.

As midnight approached, he went on deck to relieve Bottle of Beer who was on watch. Rourke was at the helm and Captain Glasscock was also on deck, sleeping on top of a hen coop. At two o'clock, Stubbs took the helm and thirty minutes later Bottle of Beer approached him. Without uttering a word, he attacked Stubbs by slashing him across the face with a cutlass. Two more blows followed, forcing Stubbs to the deck and as he lay there helpless, his attacker struck him once more, breaking his jaw. He watched Jumbo attack the captain and cut his throat, but could not see what weapon he used. Stubbs screamed 'Murder' as he crawled to the hatchway, through which he fell into the cabin below where he passed out.

When Stubbs regained consciousness, the cabin was in flames and he attempted unsuccessfully to clamber onto the deck. However, Rourke carried him up the steps where they discovered the fire raging out of control. It was obvious the vessel could not be saved and it was decided to abandon ship. The two prisoners by this time were already in one of the small boats, 700 yards away. The captain was dead and the ship's carpenter could not be found. The survivors rowed away from the sinking vessel in her other small boat, but Campigny died shortly afterwards of serious burns and his body was thrown overboard. Those remaining in the boat were Stubbs, Royal, Rourke, Griffiths, Dobie and Gould, and they were destined to spend the next seven days in the ocean before reaching land, after which they were brought back to England in different ships.

When asked if he knew of any motive for the prisoners' crimes, Stubbs replied that he had heard the captain often joke with them that he would sell them into slavery or take them to England, but he believed they did not realise, because of the language barrier, that the skipper was speaking in jest. As for their claims to have been starved, Stubbs insisted they were well fed on board the *Amelia* and were given the same food as the rest of the crew. The next witness was Rourke who said that after he was relieved by the previous witness, he went to the stern where he was sitting when he saw Bottle of Beer attacking Stubbs with the cutlass. A few minutes later he too had seen Jumbo cut the captain's throat with a sharp axe, which was usually kept by Glasscock in his cabin. Bottle of Beer rushed at the witness and slashed him twice across the face, but he managed to dash away from his attacker and alert Dobie, Royal and Griffiths who were asleep in their bunks.

At first, Royal did not believe what Rourke was telling him, but Dobie armed himself with a hammer and cutlass before making his way up the steps. He was followed by Rourke who was now similarly armed. On reaching the deck, Rourke was struck by Bottle of Beer, forcing him back into the cabin. Suddenly, there was a loud explosion and within a matter of moments, Rourke saw a fierce fire break out. On returning to the deck, Rourke was preoccupied with trying to extinguish the flames and it was some time before he saw the two prisoners rowing away from the *Amelia*.

Gould was next to stand in the witness box and he told the court of being woken up by Rourke and rushing out of the cabin to be confronted by Jumbo, who was moving away from the captain and brandishing an axe. He lunged at the witness who had a cutlass and was therefore able to defend himself and avoid injury. Gould was also able to inflict wounds to Jumbo's wrists, side and legs. He saw the captain, clutching at his bleeding throat wound, staggering across the deck. Gould watched as he fell and in so doing knock over a lamp that ignited three barrels of powder, which were stacked on the deck. There was an explosion and this was the cause of the fire that broke out almost immediately. He could see Royal attempting to sew up the captain's wound, but he could not be saved and died ten minutes later.

Dobie was too ill to give his evidence at the trial but on his arrival in Liverpool, he had described being slashed across the face by Jumbo. Royal described Bottle of Beer calling to him, 'You my friend, you save me very much. I want to talk with you.' However, Royal did not trust the African and refused to approach him. He was followed into the witness box by Griffiths and he too had been asked to talk with Bottle of Beer, but he also refused the invitation, claiming he feared he would be murdered. In common with the statements of the previous witnesses, Griffiths insisted that Captain Glasscock had treated the accused men very well and they had no cause for complaint.

Jumbo and Bottle of Beer were provided with an interpreter and when asked if they wished to say anything in their defence, they simply extended their hands and cried out, 'Not true, not true. All lies, very much lies.' It was left for their lawyer to attempt to plant seeds of doubt in the minds of the jury and when cross-examining the crew, he asked how it was that two men, inadequately armed, could overpower the other nine sailors, but he received no satisfactory answer off any of them. The jury was also reminded that the crown's witnesses had been suspected initially of responsibility for the deaths of the missing crew and had been brought back to England in chains.

Among a number of apparently insignificant inconsistencies highlighted by the defence was Gould's insistence, when questioned by the Liverpool magistrates, that Jumbo used a knife to slit the captain's throat; however, in his testimony at the trial, he was claiming an axe was used. Under cross-examination, Gould denied that he had changed his story after discussing the case with the others so that their accounts would tally. Nevertheless, when the transcript of his evidence given at Liverpool was read out, it was evident that he had said a knife was used. Gould insisted this had been a genuine error on his part. Such a discrepancy would probably have been overlooked or ignored had Jumbo and Bottle of Beer not survived, but now those thought by the defence to be the real murderers realised it was crucial for all of them to give similar accounts. This, it was proposed, confirmed that collusion had taken place and the wrong men were standing in the dock. It was also asserted that relations between the captain and the English seamen were not as harmonious as the witnesses attempted to portray. It was shown that in conversations with crewmembers of the ships bringing them home, they let slip that there were regular arguments with the skipper and that he was not a well-liked individual.

Of particular interest to the defence was that very soon into the *Amelia*'s voyage, the crew came to believe that the captain had a chest containing gold dust with an estimated value of £3,000 locked away in his cabin. When the survivors arrived on the coast of Africa, the authorities discovered that each of them was in possession of a relatively large amount of cash. The jury was reminded that none of the witnesses revealed the source of the money at the time and this was an important factor in the prisoners' defence for it was later shown that it had belonged to the captain. He was not carrying gold dust but did have a substantial sum of money with him on board; this could only have been found and shared out when his cabin was ransacked after they murdered him. The crewmembers accepted they each had almost ten pounds in cash and it did indeed belong to the captain, but they insisted they discovered it when searching for navigation aids as they were preparing to abandon the burning ship. It was not a motive for them to commit any crimes and they had not mentioned it originally because they feared by doing so they would probably have brought suspicion on themselves.

The defence was implying that some or all of the white crewmembers conspired to murder the captain and anyone who would not join them in destroying the *Amelia* and afterwards making off with the chest of gold dust they believed, wrongly, to be in Captain Glasscock's cabin. At no time following their arrests had the accused men claimed to have witnessed any of these events. This suggested the crimes occurred after Jumbo and Bottle of Beer had decided to leave the ship as they feared they were being taken to England by the captain. The crown witnesses, believing the Africans would have no chance of surviving, took the opportunity this unexpected turn of events presented them with of putting their nefarious plans into operation and later putting the blame on Jumbo and Bottle of Beer. However, having returned to Liverpool and learning that Jumbo and Bottle of Beer had survived, they lied to the Liverpool court and at the Old Bailey trial, confident their evidence would be believed over that of two black Africans, who would undoubtedly hang for crimes they had not committed.

In his summing up, the trial judge, Mr Justice Vaughn, described the case as a great mystery. He had no doubt that foul murders had been committed on board the *Amelia*, but conceded the jury might possibly have difficulty in deciding who were the real perpetrators. The jury retired and returned twenty minutes later having found the prisoners not guilty. Jumbo and Bottle of Beer were released and later found ships on which they were able to return to their homes.

No one was ever convicted of any crimes committed on board the *Amelia*.

5

The *Felicidade*, 1845

In 1807, Britain abolished the trade in slaves and with massive public support, the Royal Navy established the West Africa Squadron the following year. Its aim was to put a stop to the South Atlantic slave trade and with the end of the Napoleonic wars, the squadron was enlarged, which resulted in more than twenty ships and 2,000 men being employed in patrolling the seas between South America and West Africa. Many of the slave ships intercepted by the squadron were Brazilian.

Brazil relied heavily on slave labour, especially in its sugar plantations and following the country's independence from Portugal in 1822, the transportation of African slaves continued. Nevertheless, in 1826, Brazil signed a treaty with Great Britain and albeit reluctantly, agreed to abolish the use of slaves by 1830, in exchange for recognition by the great power and the political benefits this brought to the new nation. The terms of the treaty allowed the Royal Navy to intercept suspected Brazilian slave ships, liberate the slaves and to confiscate the vessels. Yet, Brazil failed to take any meaningful steps to reduce its dependence on slaves and the trade continued. The British declared the slave trade to be piracy and the ships of the Royal Navy were authorised to impound vessels of all nations, which were fitted out as slavers, even if when boarded they were found to be empty of a human cargo.

There were few incidents of any great significance until 26 February 1845 when HMS *Wasp*, a British cruiser on patrol in the South Atlantic, came upon a Brazilian schooner, the *Felicidade*, sailing towards the African coast. Following a brief chase, she was stopped and boarded by a party of British seamen under the command of Lieutenant R. D. Stupart. There were no slaves on board but she was clearly fitted out as a slaver. This was confirmed by her captain, Joaquim Antonio de Cuquribio, who readily acknowledged sailing out of the port of Bahia on 6 January with a crew of thirty-four, intending to return to Brazil with a cargo of slaves.

All but two of the *Felicidade*'s crew, her skipper and a seaman, Janus Majaval, were taken on board the *Wasp* and Stupart and his party were ordered to take the slaver to Freetown in Sierra Leone. However, before the two ships went their separate ways, another suspicious vessel, the *Echo*, was seen and they set off in pursuit. The *Wasp* was soon left behind but after three days, the *Echo* was finally captured by the *Felicidade* and her British crew. The suspicions of the British sailors proved to be well-founded as 430 slaves were discovered on board in appalling conditions. They were able to make themselves understood and advised Stupart they had not been provided with food or water for several days. They were overjoyed to be liberated and were informed that they would be taken back to their homeland immediately on board the *Echo* after her crew of twenty-one was transferred to the *Felicidade*, which was to resume her voyage to Freetown.

Stupart left seventeen-year-old Midshipman Thomas Palmer in command of the *Felicidade* together with nine British sailors. Those who remained with the midshipman were James Mullens, Edward Marshall, James Mitchell (all of whom were able seamen), Thomas Barfoot, James Benyon, George Godding (who were ordinary seamen) and Royal Marine Private Thomas Gould. There were also two Kroomen, known by their anglicised names of Jack Andrews and Joe Wilson, who were just two of 1,000 African fishermen recruited by the Royal Navy because of their knowledge of the seas off the West African coast.

Some hours later, Stupart was surprised to see the *Felicidade* heading towards him, the Union Jack having been lowered and the Brazilian flag hoisted once more in its place. A member of her crew, using a speaking-trumpet, shouted that she had been retaken and ordered the *Echo* to heave-to or face being fired on. The lieutenant refused to do so and ordered his crew to prepare to board the *Felicidade*. No mention had been made of his shipmates who had been left on the *Felicidade*, which was a cause of great concern to the lieutenant who hoped no harm had come to them and that they were confined below decks. Stupart intended to rescue them and realising he was not to be intimidated, the *Felicidade* decided to make for home and was soon out of sight.

Three days later, the cruiser HMS *Star* spotted the *Felicidade* and following a brief chase, was able to detain her, suspecting she was carrying slaves. The *Star*'s crew, of course, knew nothing of the events of a few days earlier, but a boarding party soon noticed fresh bloodstains on the deck. Four of the foreign crew had clearly sustained what appeared to be recently inflicted sabre wounds to their heads and faces, which they claimed had been caused when a mast fell on them. They were not believed and the British realised a serious incident of some kind must have occurred on board in the very recent past.

As he searched one of the ship's cabins, Royal Marine Corporal Thomas Lethbridge discovered a book, *Cabinet Cyclopaedia*, which bore the signature of Lieutenant Stupart on an inside page. The men on the *Felicidade* insisted initially that they could offer no explanation for the bloodstains or how the book came to be on board. Within a short time, the dreadful truth would emerge when de Cuquribio described the fate of the English sailors. They had all been murdered and despite being unable to identify them by name, he could point out their killers.

The captain revealed that within a short time of Stupart leaving the vessel, he was approached by the *Echo*'s commander, Francisco Ferreira de Santo Serva, who explained that he planned to murder the English seamen, seize control of the *Felicidade* and afterwards attempt to recapture the *Echo*. He had continued by saying, 'The Englishmen are not armed. I have four men in whom I can confide. Let us kill them all and then we will take charge of the *Echo*.' Afterwards, de Santo Serva planned to return to Rio where he would hand over the *Felicidade* to Ciudada Santo, the owner of the impounded *Echo* and if possible, his own vessel. De Cuquribio replied that if such a thing was done it would be impossible to escape from the British who would hunt them down and when taken they would be executed. De Santo Serva called him a fool and warned him not to give any warning to the British, which in retrospect de Cuquribio regretted not doing, but explained later that he did not believe anyone would be foolish enough to carry out such a plan. The account given by de Cuquribio was supported by two others. Savarina da Costa, sold as a slave when a boy and who was now a barber on the *Echo*, witnessed his captain plotting with others to seize the ship. Emmanuel Francois Rosaigro, one of de Santo Serva's servants, heard his master giving the order to attack and kill the British sailors. In common with de Cuquribio, they could not put names to the murdered men, but were able to identify the killers.

Midshipman Palmer had bathed in one of the ship's barrels and afterwards went aft where he sat down to speak with one of his shipmates. Several other British sailors were asleep on deck and it was at this moment, with their captors totally unprepared, that de Santo Serva was heard telling his men, 'Now is the time to commit the murders. The sentinel is asleep, three others are asleep and so is the one who came from the brig. There are only two men awake aft.' De Cuquribio urged them to reconsider but was threatened and his advice ignored, and he rushed aft to warn the midshipman and the sailor he was talking to.

The sailor grabbed an iron bar and rushed to the hatchway from which de Santo Serva and the others were emerging. He struck one of these men, Manuel Jose Alves, across the head and threw him overboard. He struck another three of the attackers but was overpowered and stabbed to death, his body thrown over the ship's side. Another British sailor who attempted to assist his shipmate was stabbed in the arm and still alive, he too was thrown into the sea. Janus Majaval was seen to stab the midshipman before throwing him overboard while the young Englishman was still breathing. Most of the other sailors were killed as they slept and their bodies thrown over the side, but the two Kroomen jumped overboard before they could be attacked. A mutineer approached one sailor who had managed to cling to the side of the ship who pleaded for mercy screaming, 'Don't kill me, Portuguese! Don't kill me!' However, his pleas went unanswered and his attacker stabbed him in the head, arms, hands and fingers, ensuring he lost his grip and fell to his death in the ocean. Alves had been able to clamber back on board and to continue to take part in the massacre, after which he was seen to gather up blood from the deck and drink it. The affray lasted about forty-five minutes and throughout de Santo Serva was shouting, 'Kill them! Kill them!'

Afterwards, de Santo Serva said to de Cuquribio: 'We have done the just thing in killing the English.' It was then he ordered his crew to prepare to take the *Echo*, which was approached and threatened. It quickly became clear that this would be difficult to achieve and as de Santo Serva was also concerned there might be other Royal Navy ships in the area, he decided to set a course for home. Nonetheless, the intervention of the *Star* had prevented him from reaching Brazil.

The *Echo* was already on her way to Sierra Leone where as a slaver she would be confiscated by the authorities. Lieutenant John Wilson was ordered to take the *Felicidade* there also with a crew of four ratings, three Kroomen and two prisoners; however, she was badly damaged in a fierce storm but before she sank, the crew had enough time to construct a raft. The men suffered a terrible ordeal that lasted for twenty days. A few small fish were caught and they were fortunate to catch a shark, thanks to the expertise of the Kroomen, and feed off its raw flesh and drink its blood. One of the African fishermen dived into the water and swam behind the shark as a piece of bait was held over the raft's side. When the shark rose out of the water to take the bait, the man in the water tied a rope around its tail. He next threw the other end of the rope to his companion in the raft, enabling him to drag the shark into the small craft. Nevertheless, before eventually being seen and rescued by HMS *Cygnet*, one of the British sailors, two of the Kroomen and both prisoners had perished.

Those who had been arrested and charged with murdering the British sailors were de Santo Serva and Janus Majaval, the cook on the *Felicidade* who was the only one of the accused not a member of the *Echo*'s crew. The four who had suffered sabre wounds were also incriminated and they were Manuel Jose Alves, Lorenzo Ribiero, Juan Francisco and Jose Maria Martinez. Also named by the witnesses were Antonio Joaquim, Sebastian de Santos, Manuel Antonio and Jose Antonio.

The accused were taken to England and appeared before Mr Baron Platt at the Exeter Assizes on 24 July. As they were Portuguese and Spanish speaking, a Mr Bellamy of Plymouth acted as interpreter. In line with custom, as the accused did not speak English, a jury comprising half-English and half-foreign nationals was selected, which was known as a 'jury de mediatate linguae' or a jury of the half tongue. At the conclusion of three days' evidence, the most crucial of which was provided by the three Brazilian slavers who testified on behalf of the crown, seven of the defendants were found guilty and sentenced to death. de Santos, Alves and Jose Antonio were cleared of any involvement and released.

During the trial, the defence lawyers argued that the British courts had no right to put the accused on trial as the alleged crimes took place on a Brazilian ship, which the Royal Navy had no right to detain when it became clear to the officers that there were no slaves on board. It was claimed that according to international law, the British sailors were acting as pirates and the condemned men were acting legitimately in defending themselves and the vessel. Nevertheless, the jury had accepted the crown's case that the *Felicidade* was seized legally as it was undoubtedly a slaver. However, the trial judge acknowledged that there were important legal issues that should be addressed and on 15 November, the case was brought before Lord Denman and a panel of senior judges at the Court of Exchequer in London. After deliberating for three weeks and by a narrow majority, the court found in favour of the defence. Accordingly, the prisoners were released and handed over to the Brazilian authorities and arrangements were made to take them home, the costs of which were borne by the British government.

The decision was praised throughout the world and enhanced Britain's reputation as a country in which the rule of law was of paramount importance. At home, it was widely condemned as it called into question the government's commitment to protect members of the Royal Navy who were regularly called upon to put their lives at risk for their country. It was said that afterwards, when boarding slave ships, British sailors would cry, 'Remember the *Felicidade*.' The crews of seized vessels were often cast adrift in small boats with little hope of survival or left without arms and provisions along the West African coastline where they would be slaughtered by local villagers.

6

The *Martha and Jane*, 1857

It was the summer of 1856 when the *Martha and Jane*, a Sunderland-registered barque, sailed out of Hartlepool to begin her voyage to Calcutta. By April of the following year, she was in Demerara, taking on board a cargo of sugar, before setting sail for Liverpool; however, the vessel sprang a leak and made for Barbados where repairs were carried out and there was also a change of captain and crew. The new skipper was thirty-seven-year-old Henry Rogers, a native of Sunderland although his home was now in Swansea where his wife and five children were living.

Rogers was an experienced and widely respected seaman who began his career as an able seaman in the Royal Navy on the seventy-four gun HMS *Russell*. He was discharged from the service at Sheerness four years later with a Certificate of Good Conduct and immediately joined the merchant navy. He was soon promoted to mate and subsequently skippered several ships, most recently the *Sybil*, the *Tartar* and the *Deptford*. His first task as skipper of the *Martha and Jane* was to recruit a crew. Twenty-seven-year-old William Miles was taken on as first mate and Charles Seymour, who was twenty-five, came aboard as second mate. Seven seamen, a steward, cook, a cabin boy and carpenter also joined the barque for the voyage to England. On 29 April, one of the first seamen to be taken on board was thirty-two-year-old Scotsman Andrew Rose, a simple-minded individual who, it was realised early into the voyage, was suffering from poor physical health.

Francis Doyle joined the ship on the same day as Rose and within the first few hours, he witnessed the second mate beating Rose with a thick rope, claiming he had failed to carry out an order satisfactorily. This treatment continued for several days and the captain and first mate also beat him. The *Martha and Jane* had not yet left port, but Rose had already had enough and said to Doyle, 'I will go ashore. I will not be treated like this.' He left in one of the *Martha and Jane*'s small boats, but was brought back to the ship by a constable on the eve of the barque leaving Barbados and Captain Rogers ordered that Rose be put in irons overnight.

Rose, it must be said, did not endear himself to his shipmates as he behaved oddly on a number of occasions, such as when he babbled incoherently or sang hymns at the top of his voice. The situation was made worse as he seemed incapable of keeping himself clean. He suffered badly from diarrhoea and began to take the shirts of other crewmembers to clean himself. As a result of this behaviour, Rose was struck by some of the crew, including William Groves, Nathaniel Martin and Francis Doyle, but these were isolated incidents. However, his lack of even the most basic standards of hygiene meant that he soon began to smell badly, which led the other seamen to refuse to let him sleep with them in the forecastle. He therefore had to sleep on deck at night.

From the very start of the voyage, Rose was treated with great brutality on a daily basis by Rogers, Miles and Seymour. Initially, the other crewmembers considered this harsh treatment by the senior officers to be justified because it was thought Rose was lazy and often insubordinate, but it soon became evident that if he was given a little leeway and additional time, Rose was able to perform the duties of a merchant seaman to a satisfactory standard. Nevertheless, the beatings continued and grew even more brutal and by this time, the rest of the crew had come to believe the punishment was excessive and not deserved. Rose was often beaten by the captain as many as six times in a day. Rogers used his own whip and the mates beat him with lengths of rope. On one occasion, he was beaten so savagely on his back and shoulders that the shirt was ripped from his body. The three officers made no attempt to hide what they did from the crew and a pattern was soon established whereby the captain would whip the unfortunate man – this served as a signal to the mates to beat him afterwards. On one occasion, Seymour ordered Rose to splice an eye in a rope and when he failed to complete the task in good time, he beat him about the head and body with his fists. Rose was helpless against the three officers, but one time he was heard to shout at Rogers, 'I'll make you sweat for this when we get back to England.' The irate captain responded by screaming at the mate, 'Mr Seymour, do you hear what the fellow says? Come here and give him some more so that you may have something to pay for.' The savagery continued.

The captain had a dog called Watch and many times the crew watched helplessly as Rogers gave it the command to attack Rose by shouting 'Bite that man.' Watch would also bite Rose when it saw his master begin to whip him. He was frequently attacked in this manner when in irons on the deck, unable to move or to defend himself. Very soon into the voyage, large pieces of flesh had been taken from all over his body.

The cruelty took many forms and for most of the time Rose was fed on bread and water only. One day, a sympathetic shipmate managed to feed him a little rice, but was ordered to stop or face severe punishment himself. Another time, Rose was forced to run up and down the rigging naked, a humiliating and painful experience. Once, when in irons on the deck, he began to sing his favourite hymn, 'Oh be Joyful', causing the captain to give the order 'Gag that man.' His hands were tied behind his back and the mates produced a large rusty iron bolt that was forced into his mouth to prevent him from singing. He suffered this agonising ordeal for more than an hour before the bolt was removed.

One particularly appalling act of cruelty occurred when Captain Rogers and the mates put Rose into an empty water barrel. The space was too small for him to stand upright and he was forced into a crouching position. The top was fastened down and there was only a small bunghole through which he was able to breathe. The officers enjoyed themselves by rolling the barrel up and down the deck for some time, ignoring the pitiful cries from inside. Afterwards, the barrel was lashed to the ship's side which was accompanied by a threat from the captain to put in irons any man who attempted to provide Rose with food or water. Nevertheless, Groves was able to give him a little water and Doyle passed some pea soup to him without either man being seen by the ship's officers. Rose was released from his prison after being in the barrel for an agonising twelve hours.

The inability of Rose to control his bowel movements had already created difficulties with his fellow seamen, which led to several of them striking him and refusing to allow him to sleep with them in the forecastle. However, his shipmates were disgusted at the treatment meted out to him on two occasions when Rose, wearing only a flannel shirt and in irons, defecated on the deck. The first time it happened, Rogers ordered seamen Doyle and James Cahill to pin Rose down by holding his arms and legs. He next gathered up the excrement on the end of a stick and forced it into the poor wretch's nostrils and mouth. Rogers taunted him by saying, 'Isn't it nice? You shall have more of it.' The second time Rose failed to control himself, Rogers inflicted a similar punishment.

The final and possibly most barbaric act took place in the first week of June and was witnessed by everyone on board the *Martha and Jane*. Rogers approached his victim and shouted, 'I wish you would jump overboard or hang yourself.' Rose replied, 'Why don't you do it for me?' Accusing him of insolence, Rogers called on the mates to help him carry Rose to the main mast. A rope was found and the captain tied a timber hitch with which to create a noose, which he placed around Rose's neck. He was lifted three feet off the deck and was left suspended for two minutes. His face turned black, his eyes protruded from their sockets and he began to froth at the mouth. When cut down, Rose smashed against the deck so hard that he bit through his tongue. He was insensible and was taken to the forecastle by another member of the crew where it was hoped he would find shelter and some relief from this torment.

Forty-eight hours later, Rogers ordered that Rose, who had lost his speech and could not stand unaided, should be brought to him. He was a pitiful sight and Rogers may well have realised he was close to death. Possibly in the hope of saving his life, Rogers gave him some brandy and castor oil. Rose was left to sleep on the deck overnight and the next morning, Rogers gave him a repeat dose. However, it was far too late and Rose died ten minutes later at ten o'clock. The corpse was badly swollen and covered with massive bruises and open wounds, which had been caused by the thrashings and dog bites, and in which maggots could be seen crawling. The captain ordered that the corpse should be brought to the side of the ship but as the crew were reluctant to touch it, the dead man was dragged there by a rope that was tied around his shoulders. Rogers then ordered that the body be thrown overboard, which was done without a prayer or any other words being spoken. The *Martha and Jane* was 200 miles off Cape Clear and only days from home. Rose would, of course, be unable to carry through with his promise to make Captain Rogers 'Sweat in England' for his sadism, but his shipmates would at least try and do so on his behalf.

Many of the crew realised they emerged from the voyage with little credit. Some had struck him and all had stood by without intervening to prevent the ill treatment. Their assaults were isolated incidents in response to particular acts such as when he took their clothes to clean himself. Furthermore, they had felt unable to step in and prevent the maltreatment as they feared brutal retribution from the ship's officers. Nevertheless, despite not knowing how the authorities ashore would view their culpability, all of the ship's hands reported the circumstances surrounding the death of Rose to the police as soon as the ship reached Liverpool.

William Groves had kept a daily log of the brutal treatment suffered by Rose, which he handed to the investigating officers. Further information was provided by Francis Doyle, William Richardson, Isaac Braithwaite, Nathaniel Martin, Thomas Heyes, William Power and Thomas Kennedy, all of whom expressed a willingness to testify on behalf of the crown at a trial. On 12 June, Detective John Eaton of the Liverpool police arrested the three officers on suspicion of murder. Miles and Seymour said nothing but Rogers said he was expecting to be detained. He explained that he had been informed by a third party that Groves was going to report him as he hoped to receive a daily payment of ten shillings for acting as a prosecution witness at a trial.

No other crewmember was accused of involvement in the murder of Rose and the trial of the three prisoners opened in St George's Hall, Liverpool, on 20 August. The Attorney General led for the crown and Rogers was represented by Mr Monk QC. Mr Aspinall spoke on behalf of Miles and Seymour who argued they were simply following the captain's orders. The crown, however, refused to accept such a claim as any order had to be lawful and all three defendants were viewed as being equally guilty of a catalogue of terrible and unlawful violence against a helpless individual who had been singled out for harsh treatment.

An attempt was made by the defence to suggest that the court had no authority to hear the case as it was claimed the *Martha and Jane* was not a British ship. Proof of ownership and registration in this country was produced and although the alleged crime was committed on the high seas, it occurred on a British ship and the victim was a British subject, which meant the court did have jurisdiction. As there was no body, the crown was required to prove a murder had taken place. Accordingly, three surgeons – Mr Desmond, Mr Pennington and Mr Wall – testified that if the evidence of the seamen was correct, the actions of the three prisoners would have caused the death of Rose and a murder would have been committed.

The defence lawyers argued that although it was not immediately obvious when he was taken on as a member of the crew, Rose was in poor physical health and insane. It was emphasised that the crew even refused to allow him to sleep with them and had beaten him on a number of occasions. As for the log written by Groves, this was described as fiction, designed with the intention of protecting him and his shipmates from any blame. Captain Rogers, it was said, was a man of integrity, who with his two senior officers had acted solely to maintain discipline. The jury was also reminded that the captain administered brandy and medicine to Rose when it became clear to him that his health was deteriorating badly. If the jury believed the prisoners were guilty of a criminal act it was only of assault and not murder.

In his address to the jury, the judge said it was essential that in a maritime nation such as Britain, its seamen had to know that no matter how far they were from their homes and families, they were protected by the country's laws. He added that a vessel's captain should have the power to supress any form of insubordination and to maintain discipline, but his actions must fall within the limits of the law. The jury left to consider its verdict and returned forty-five minutes later. The foreman revealed they had concluded that Rose died as a result of the cruelty of the three accused, but wished to have the difference between murder and manslaughter explained to them. This was done by the judge and the jury retired once again. Ten minutes later, the jury returned with guilty verdicts of murder in respect of the three defendants but added recommendations of mercy for them all, which the judge promised to send to the Home Secretary. The verdicts and the subsequent death sentences were greeted with loud and sustained cheering by the crowds gathered outside the court building.

Reading the newspapers of the day, it is clear that the convictions were welcomed as it was widely believed that many sea captains abused their powers and an example had to be made. *The Times* welcomed the verdicts and sentences but in common with most of the press, was appalled that the jury recommended that mercy should be shown to the culprits. An editorial commented: 'The Liverpool jury no sooner pronounce their verdict than they start back from the sound themselves have made and recommend the criminals to mercy. But what can be the meaning of such a recommendation? If this is wilful murder, surely it is one of the most atrocious and revolting ever committed?' The *Daily News* had no sympathy whatsoever with the perpetrators and was against mercy being extended to them. Its outraged editor observed: 'There is no body of men more liable to gross tyranny and brutal violence than the mariners in our merchant service; there is none whose safety and comfort ought to be an object of such paramount care to the government of the greatest maritime and mercantile community in the world.'

The *Leeds Mercury* opposed mercy and reflected public concern noting: 'There have been too many cases like that of Anthony Rose lately; justice calls loudly for an example and no more fitting examples can be offered at her shrine than the three wretches who on Thursday last received sentence of death at Liverpool.' The *Morning Post* welcomed the verdicts but was not so critical of the jury's recommendation for mercy. The editor hoped the outcome would put an end to 'The brutalities which we regret to say are now so frequently committed at sea by ships' captains upon their crews, or as it usually happens, upon some unhappy individual of that crew, who with or without reason, may have incurred the dislike of the master.'

The three prisoners shared the condemned cell in the Kirkdale House of Correction, in which they were visited daily by the prison's chaplain, Reverenced Richard Appleton. Despite almost universal antipathy towards them, efforts were being made to secure reprieves. A solicitor, Mr Snowball, took the train to London and spent one-and-a-half hours with Sir George Grey, the Home Secretary, who decided that Miles and Seymour were to be reprieved and transported to Australia for life as it was acknowledged they were under some pressure to obey the captain's orders. However, the minister was far less sympathetic as far as Rogers was concerned and he could not be saved from the hangman's noose. His hanging was set for noon on 12 September.

Miles and Seymour were told of their reprieves on 9 September when prison officers came to take them out of the condemned cell and transfer them to the main prison. Nevertheless, they sought permission to remain with their captain for a few hours longer and the governor agreed to their request. The three friends spent their time together in prayer and reminiscing about life at sea. Two days later on the eve of his execution, Rogers received his final visit from his wife and three eldest children, which proved to be a moving and distressing experience for the family and staff. Mrs Rogers returned to Swansea with the children that night.

One of the doomed man's final acts was to write the following letter to a friend:

Kirkdale Gaol, Sept 11, 1857.

My dear fellow, I duly received your kind and welcome letter of the 7th instant and thank you for the trouble you have taken on my account. I am happy to say the mates have got their lives spared; they have got transported for life but there is no hope for me. But, my dear fellow, I shall die an innocent man and I hope and trust that God will receive my soul. I am more than obliged to you for the advice I received from you in godly affairs. Mrs Rogers has been almost every day to see me; but this day I take my farewell, and my poor children, may God be a father to them. We had prayer yesterday and today; we take the sacrament together. And may God bless her and them in this world. My dear fellow, I have not neglected my prayers since I have been condemned and if God will accept them I hope to be happy in the next world. But it seems to me like a dream and I think the reason is that I know I am not guilty of the crime. This God knows. You wish to know how I am. Sometimes I am ready to burst with grief and there are times I am quite resigned to my fate. I think I should have died had not Mrs Rogers been here, but, poor thing, she has kept up my failing heart. The officers and governor have been very kind to me, more than any man could expect and I am very thankful for their kindness. I have had more comfort than ever I thought to obtain but God is good. I have another good friend and that is the chaplain; he is very kind. Both he and the governor have been more than I can say. I hope the Lord will bless them for their kindness to me and my poor wife and children. You must consider that I am in this gaol a condemned prisoner and death is my fate, although not guilty of the crime charged. You say in yours that there has been a memorial from Liverpool, but that I sent myself, and the reply was the jury found me guilty and I must suffer. My lawyer went to London and saw Sir George Grey and laid all things before him and they said as the jury had found me guilty I must suffer death, so God receive my poor soul. I must conclude. By the time you get this I shall be no more. I am thankful they have spared the lives of my poor mates. So now, my dear fellow, God bless you and all your family, as this is my last letter in this world. But I hope to meet you in the world to come, where no person can swear anybody's life away. But I forgive them, as I hope to be forgiven myself. So goodbye and the Almighty be with you. I remain my dear fellow, yours truly and not guilty.

HENRY ROGERS

On the Friday evening, Rogers was visited in his cell by Thomas Wright, Manchester's famous prison philanthropist. Wright visited many condemned prisoners to offer support and comfort and if the prisoner agreed, he would accompany him or her on to the scaffold and Rogers agreed he could do so. The condemned man is reported to have slept relatively well for a few hours but was awake at five o'clock and breakfasted on a little milk.

Executions were still performed in public but much of the ritual had been dispensed with. The scaffold was draped in black cloth so that only the upper bodies of the prisoner and the accompanying officials were visible. The hanging was due to take place at noon outside the main gate and many people began to gather six hours earlier in order to find a good vantage point. As the numbers of spectators grew throughout the morning, reporters noted many sailors in the crowd who expressed regret that the two mates were not standing alongside their captain. As the prison clock struck noon, the traditional cry of 'Hats off' came from among the crowd that was estimated at between 30,000-60,000 men, women and children. They fell silent as Rogers, Mr Wright, the governor and chaplain, together with the hangman William Calcraft, walked out onto the gallows. They watched as Calcraft adjusted the noose around the murderer's neck and pulled the white cap down over his face. Rogers was heard to say 'Lord Jesus, receive my spirit. Lord save me,' before falling through the drop. After an hour, the body was cut down and Rogers was buried within the precincts of the gaol.

It was reported later that the owner of Allsop's Waxwork Exhibition on Lime Street in Liverpool visited the gaol on the Saturday morning. He had an interview with the under-sheriff and sought permission to take a cast of the condemned man's head. This request was refused but Mr Allsop was allowed to observe him from a distance and to make several sketches. It was customary to allow the hangman to keep the condemned prisoner's clothes following an execution and Calcraft agreed to sell those belonging to Rogers to Mr Allsop.

Three days after the execution, an advertisement appeared in the local press announcing that the waxwork models of Rogers, Miles and Seymour were on public display. It added that the captain's model was wearing the clothes worn at his hanging.

7

The *Coldbeck*, 1875

Eight years had passed since the last execution took place outside the walls of Kirkdale House of Correction and although now carried out in private, crowds still gathered at the main gate when a hanging was due to take place. The morning of 6 September 1875 was no exception and the day was rather special as two men were to be hanged simultaneously. William Baker had been convicted of shooting Charles Langan on London Road in Liverpool and the man who would be standing next to him on the gallows was thirty-three-year-old Edward Cooper who had been found guilty of murdering Edward Jones on board the cargo ship *Coldbeck*. The crowd could be numbered in dozens rather than in the thousands of previous executions, but the sellers of broadsides continued to peddle their wares, one of which, published by White, a local printer, read as follows:

> Within the walls of Kirkdale prison,
> Edward Cooper, a seaman, he
> Is doomed to die for wilful murder
> Which he committed on the high sea,
> On a British vessel named the *Coldbeck*.
> Cooper and the boatswain had words and strife,
> When Edward Cooper fired a revolver
> And cruelly took the boatswain's life.
>
> None to pity him, sad and friendless,
> In Kirkdale prison now does lie,
> Poor Edward Cooper, a British seaman
> For wilful murder condemned to die.

It was on the 24th of April,
While the *Coldbeck* was outward bound
Poor Edward Jones who was the boatswain,
That day received his death wound.
Without provocation and without warning,
His crimson blood did stain the deck;
By a pistol shot from Edward Cooper,
He lost his life on the *Coldbeck*.

Then Edward Cooper was put in irons,
And sent back to Liverpool with speed,
Before Justice Archibald at the assizes,
He had to answer for the wicked deed.

He was found guilty and the sentence
Was passed as each one held his breath,
They told him for the crime of murder
The dreaded penalty was death.

He lies, his dreadful fate awaiting,
Heaven knows what he must feel,
His thoughts must drive him to distraction,
As the fleeting hours from him sleet.
He soon must stand upon the scaffold,
And to eternity be hurled,
And by the hands of the common hangman,
Be launched into another world.

Let Cooper's fate then be a warning,
To revengeful passion don't give way.
All angry feeling pray be scorning,
Or you'll regret it some fatal day.
God forgive the sinful murderer,
As his moments quickly roll,
And when the grave receives his body,
May Heaven receive his precious soul.

Cooper's crime and the circumstances leading up to it were described during his trial at the Liverpool Assizes on 14 August. The *Coldbeck* sailed out of Liverpool in the early spring of 1875 bound for Valparaiso.

Within a few days, it became evident to the rest of the crew that there was a great deal of bad blood between Cooper, who was an able seaman and Edward Jones, the ship's boatswain. They appeared to have taken an instant dislike to each other, Cooper resenting what he felt was the other's overbearing attitude and Jones believing Cooper was not performing his duties adequately.

They argued repeatedly and on 20 April there was a particularly unpleasant confrontation in the sail room, which was witnessed by Thomas Gibson, the *Coldbeck*'s sail maker. Cooper walked into the room and a few minutes later he was followed by the boatswain. Angry words passed between them but Gibson did not know the reason. Jones left and Cooper also walked out and as he did so, turned to Gibson and said he would soon return. On doing so a few minutes later, the sail maker was shocked when Cooper produced a revolver, which he was invited to examine and Gibson noticed there was a bullet in each of the weapon's six chambers. Cooper uttered no direct threat against the boatswain, but the sail maker sensed the malice that was present in his voice when speaking of the other man.

It was approaching five-thirty on 24 April and the sail maker was in the forecastle with several members of the crew, including Cooper, who was drinking a cup of tea. Jones entered and shouted out an order to Cooper, demanding that he 'Come and help us haul the mizzen middle staysail up.' Jones left but Cooper did not follow him and remained seated, sipping his tea. Jones returned and now furious repeated the order, reminding Cooper that as he was on watch, it was his duty to help with the task. Cooper did not move but simply laughed out loud, which led Jones to threaten to report him to the captain, shouting 'You have had your way long enough.' At this, Cooper stood and put his face close to that of his adversary in a menacing manner. Sensing trouble, the others left the forecastle, which meant Cooper and Jones were now on their own.

At first, all was quiet but then the boatswain was heard to say 'Put that revolver away. Come on deck and fight like a man.' In reply, Cooper shouted 'I'll shoot you' and this threat was followed by the sound of a single gunshot. Jones staggered out of the forecastle clutching his chest. He fell and murmured 'May the Lord have mercy on my soul. I'm done for.' He was carried into the captain's cabin where he died a few minutes later. The captain assembled the crew and demanded to know from Cooper if he was responsible for shooting Jones. He replied, 'Yes and I knew it would happen as soon as Jones was put in charge.' He was advised by the captain that he would be detained on suspicion of murder and that the ship would alter course and return to Liverpool. Cooper held up his thumb that was bleeding and said, 'Captain, he cut me and I had to do it.' The captain ordered a thorough search be made of the ship, but no knife that the dead man could have used to injure Cooper in such a manner was found.

Having heard the evidence, the jury did not accept the suggestion that Cooper had acted in self-defence or that he could be convicted of the lesser charge of manslaughter on the grounds of provocation. He was convicted of wilful murder but the jury added a strong recommendation for mercy. There was a great deal of sympathy for the convicted man and there were serious misgivings about the quality of his representation at the trial, which were expressed in the following letter published in the *Liverpool Mercury*:

Gentlemen, a friend of mine had an interview yesterday with the convict Edward Cooper, now awaiting execution in Kirkdale Gaol. Cooper then said that he had no communication with the counsel who defended him on his trial until he was in the dock. There has not been time to verify this statement but it is one which, made as it was quietly without excitement, deserves attention. The man was brought to Liverpool to be tried for his life. He arrives here friendless, he is extremely ignorant and has no relations to advise with him. He is poor and unable to obtain adequate legal assistance. The judge (as I presume, without having been able to inquire into all the facts) did all for him that could be done, by requesting one of the barristers in attendance at the court to undertake the case. Now it may well be doubted whether a criminal in the hands of even the acutest lawyer would have much chance under such circumstances.

The barrister is called upon to defend a man's life without having had any previous communication with him or any time for reflection on the points of the evidence. Could there be any wonder if, under such circumstances some point should be overlooked which, if brought into sufficient prominence, would have the effect of altering the nature of the crime charged against the prisoner? Has this man had that fair play – that fair chance of his life which Englishmen feel is the right of even the greatest criminals? Can it be right that in such a case an irrevocable sentence should be carried out? Cooper has had no hint that any attempt is being made to have his case mercifully looked at; but surely when the Liverpool public are made aware of the circumstances, they will shrink from allowing him to be hung, without an appeal for mercy being laid before the crown.

D. A. Fox
Water Street
August 28th 1875

A well-supported petition seeking a reprieve was organised by the staff and residents of the Liverpool Sailors' Home in which the condemned man had sometimes lodged and where he was known by his peers to be an excellent seaman. He was an American, originally from New Orleans, where his parents still lived and he had run away to sea when just a boy. He settled in Liverpool and was employed regularly by Messrs Fergusons, ship owners of South Castle Street, who now offered him their full support. Most importantly, the petition was signed by several members of the jury that convicted him. Nevertheless, there was to be no reprieve and the following letter, dated 3 September, was received from the Home Office by the Secretary of the Liverpool Sailor's Home:

> Sir, with reference to your application on behalf of Edward Cooper, now under sentence of death in the county prison at Kirkdale, I am directed by Mr Secretary Cross to acquaint you that after full inquiry and consideration of all the circumstances of the case, he has been unable to find any sufficient grounds to justify him, consistently with his public duty, in recommending Her Majesty's interference with the due course of law – I am sir, your obedient servant.

> A. F. O. Liddell

William Baker was unable to sleep on the eve of his execution, but Cooper slept well and was woken up by the warders at six o'clock. After eating a light breakfast, the condemned men were visited by their respective religious advisers who remained with them until the end. At quarter to eight, the prison bell began to toll, indicating that the executions were imminent. The Home Office had for many years been determined to prevent the attendance of the press on such occasions, but that would take several years to achieve. For this double event, the number of journalists allowed to enter the execution chamber was restricted to five.

At eight o'clock, the two prisoners, already pinioned, approached the gallows. Baker was pale and clearly terrified, but Cooper walked firmly onto the drop. Before the white cap was pulled down over his head and the noose placed around his neck, the American turned to the members of the press and said in a firm voice, 'All I can say is that I have not had justice.' William Marwood was the executioner and he performed his task in his usual calm, dignified and professional manner, treating both men, who died instantly, with great compassion throughout their ordeal.

Cooper had not visited his family for several years and as he was illiterate, he asked his priest to write to his parents in New Orleans to advise them of his fate. Following the inquest held later that afternoon, Cooper and Baker were buried in the prison grounds.

8

The *Lennie*, 1875

It was October 1875 and the English-owned barque *Lennie*, which was registered in the port of Yarmouth, Nova Scotia, was berthed in Amsterdam, preparing to sail across the Atlantic. Her skipper was Stanley Hatfield, a French Canadian, and his senior officers were English. Joseph Wortley was the chief mate and the second mate was Richard MacDonald. Captain Hatfield had no other crewmembers until 22 October when Constant Von Hoydonck, a twenty-five-year-old Belgian, came on board as chief steward and sixteen-year-old Henry Troussilot, a native of Holland, was hired as cabin boy.

Two days later, the owner's agent arrived with eleven crewmembers who had signed the required documents in London. There were eight Greeks: Giovanni Moros, Mateo Cargalis alias French Peter, Giovanni Cacaris alias Joe the Cook, Paroscos Leosis, Pascalis Caludis alias Big Harry, George Kaida alias Lips, George Angelos also known as Little George and Giovanni Kenesa. Charles Renken was English, Giuseppe Lettis was an Austrian and Peter Petersen a Dane. Captain Hatfield was concerned that there were so many foreigners and foresaw possible difficulties if he could not make his commands understood. It was therefore agreed with the agent that Kenesa, who spoke several languages and could translate the captain's and mates' orders, would act as boatswain for an additional monthly payment of thirty shillings. The ship sailed later that day and the first week of the voyage was incident free. However, shocking crimes would soon take place and those responsible were brought to trial, due to the tenacity and courage of the steward who was assisted by the cabin boy.

In the early hours of 31 October, Von Hoydonck was asleep in his bunk when he was woken up by loud voices coming from the deck above his head. He heard the captain shouting out an order and swearing at the crew. A few moments later all went quiet, but the steward sensed there was trouble after hearing the captain begin to moan. Troussilot was sleeping close by and he too was woken up by the disturbance. They both attempted to open the hatchway, but it was fastened down and they were unable to open it fully. Nonetheless, they managed to prise it open a little, but they were seen doing so by Caludis and Kaida who ordered them to close it and to return to their bunks. The steward and cabin boy were able to gain access to the officers' cabin where they discovered two loaded pistols, which Von Hoydonck put in his pockets, sensing he might need them later. The skylight too was fastened down but he managed to catch a glimpse of Renken standing at the wheel and a few minutes later, Von Hoydonck and Troussilot heard several gunshots.

At ten minutes to six, they were allowed out and although he had not witnessed any violence, the steward's worst fears appeared to be confirmed. There was no sign of the captain and mates and the main deck was covered in blood, which Caludis, Cargalis, Cacaris and Leosis were attempting to scrub clean. The ship's name was painted in gilt on either side of the bow, on the stern and on her small boats. Von Hoydonck noticed Kaida and Angelos painting over these, thereby removing all traces of the *Lennie*'s identity. Later, he watched as a number of the Greeks ransacked the officers' chests for anything of value. Caludis announced that he would henceforth be wearing the captain's uniform and be sleeping in what used to be his cabin. Kenesa told Von Hoydonck, 'Well, steward, we have finished now. We have finished the captain, mate and second mate.' He realised what was meant by this and knew the three men were dead and that their bodies must have been thrown into the sea.

Von Hoydonck and Troussilot now feared for their lives but it became obvious none of the mutineers knew how to navigate the ship and they were aware the steward was able to. It was Kenesa who revealed the mutineers' plans to him. Von Hoydonck was to take the *Lennie* to Gibraltar and from there the mutineers intended sailing her to Greece where the ship would be stripped of everything that could be sold and afterwards scuttled. Kenesa said he and Moros were cousins and their uncle was a wealthy ship owner who would gladly purchase the rigging, sails and navigation aids and the proceeds would be shared out among the crew. Kenesa assured the steward that his uncle would employ him as a captain of one of his ships as a reward for the help he was now giving. Von Hoydonck knew very well that he had no alternative other than to do as he was asked, but he insisted that the crew gave an undertaking to obey his orders without question. They agreed after he explained that without their total obedience it would be impossible to reach the Mediterranean.

On every day of the voyage, Von Hoydonck had helped the captain set the *Lennie*'s course so he knew her current position, which was about 180 miles from Falmouth. He gave the order that the ship was to be made ready to continue on her way, but Von Hoydonck had no intention of joining the conspiracy and unbeknown to the others he set a course for the Bristol Channel; however, he was playing a dangerous game and after three days had passed, Renken was at the wheel with him. He turned to Von Hoydonck and said, 'You are not going to Gibraltar, you are going to the Channel. I can tell by the water.' Von Hoydonck replied curtly, 'You mind your business, I am master now. I have got charge of the ship. If you don't keep quiet and civil I will blow your brains out.' Renken was later relieved by Petersen but the Englishman was far from satisfied with Von Hoydonck's response. The steward heard him say to some of the others, 'He is going to sell us. He is not going to Gibraltar. He is going to the Channel!' A group approached Von Hoydonck menacingly and he was relieved that he had let it be known he was armed. Caludis asked the steward for an assurance that the ship was heading towards the Mediterranean and he and the others seemed content to accept his word that he was indeed taking the ship to Gibraltar.

Nevertheless, the incident caused Von Hoydonck to change his plans and instead of making for the Bristol Channel, he altered course for the French coast as that was nearer. The only person he felt he could trust was Troussilot and confided in him. He knew the cabin boy could speak French and asked him to write twenty-four notes in that language, which were to be put in sealed bottles and thrown overboard secretly in the hope at least one of them might be found on the shore and passed to the relevant authorities. Each one of them read as follows:

Please send as quick as possible plenty of police, tow boat and men because the sailors have killed the captain, mate and second mate. We left Antwerp for New York on the 23rd and the mutiny was on the 31st. Ship is three mast named *Lennie* of Yarmouth; Captain Hatfield. Please keep policemen below so that we may save our lives.

Constant Von Hoydonck, Steward.

On the night of 4 November, Cacaris was on watch with Von Hoydonck. The Greek turned to him and said, 'Don't you be afraid, they won't kill you. They won't do you any harm as long as you see us right to Greece. We have done enough. We have killed three and we don't want to do no more. But I am afraid they will kill the boy because they are afraid when he comes ashore in Greece or anywhere, he will split upon them and tell the tale.' Von Hoydonck attempted to reassure Cacaris telling him, 'I will make sure he will say nothing. It is only his first voyage at sea. Leave him alone.' Later, Cargalis and Caludis approached him and said, 'All right, steward, we can trust you. You promise he won't say nothing when he gets ashore. You look out that everything will be right won't you?' Von Hoydonck assured them that Troussilot would not pose any problems.

However, it became clear the following day that Cargalis was no longer so certain that Von Hoydonck could be trusted and threatened him saying, 'I will have to do with you the same as I have done with the others. You will sell us all.' The steward was concerned that one of the leaders of the mutiny was losing faith in him, but decided to take a calculated risk. He replied that as Cargalis and the others seemed to have little faith in him, he was no longer prepared to navigate the ship. Petersen volunteered to replace him but proved to be hopeless at the task. On the evening of the sixth, Caludis asked the steward to resume responsibility for navigating the ship but he refused. A few hours later, Caludis, who was now accompanied by Cacaris, Leosis and Renken, pleaded with him to change his mind. More confident of the strength of his position, the steward agreed but insisted he was not to be challenged again and he promised to take them to Gibraltar. Caludis turned to the others and warned them that if any man interfered in any way with the steward, he would slice off his ears.

On the evening of the seventh and now in sight of the French coast, Von Hoydonck ordered the crew to drop anchor, telling them they were close to Cadiz and when there was sufficient wind they would be able to reach Gibraltar. At five o'clock in the morning, he threw more bottles into the sea containing messages seeking urgent assistance. He also hoisted the flag that signalled 'ship in distress' but this was seen and pulled down three hours later by Cargalis and Petersen who told Von Hoydonck they were doing so as they were unsure of its meaning.

Later that day, a French pilot boat sailed out of St-Martin-de-Re and saw the *Lennie* at anchor. Her skipper noticed the absence of any identifying marks and sailed to within hailing distance. Cargalis advised the French vessel that they were waiting for a fair wind and would then continue their journey. However, this failed to satisfy the pilot and on returning to port, the crew reported their suspicions and the gunboat *Travailleur* was sent to investigate.

Having realised Von Hoydonck had betrayed them and that they were lying off the coast of France and faced the possibility of being arrested, Cargalis, Cacaris, Leosis, Caludis, Kaida and Renken decided to row for shore in one of the *Lennie*'s small boats, taking with them what valuables they could carry. After they left the ship, Von Hoydonck showed his hand and pulled out one of the pistols, informing those who remained on board that he was taking another of the small boats to row over to the French gunboat. Having heard his account of the murders, the *Travailleur*'s captain sent a party of five sailors to secure the *Lennie*, which was towed to Rochefort. All of those on board, except for the cabin boy, were arrested by the French police immediately they stepped ashore.

The mutiny had been discovered before any of the bottles containing the messages were found. Nevertheless, they were of great significance, for as they began to be washed up along the French coastline, they served to prove the innocence of Von Hoydonck and Troussilot. Also of importance were the offers of Lettis and Petersen to testify against those they claimed were guilty of plotting the mutiny and of murdering the ship's officers. The steward and cabin boy were confined to their cabin when the murders took place and could not give an eyewitness account of what occurred. Lettis and Petersen, however, had been on deck and they provided a graphic description of what took place.

At midnight on the night in question, Lettis went on watch with the chief mate, Kenesa, Angelos, Renken, Kaida and Moros. At about three-thirty, Captain Hatfield came on deck as he wished to alter course and called on those due to take over on the next watch to come and assist. All of the crew, except for the steward and cabin boy were soon on deck. The skipper shouted out the order, 'Bout ship, main topsail all. Haul away the main braces, you sons of bitches, sons of whores.' However, his order was not followed. Lettis saw Caludis lunge at the captain and stab him in the stomach, forcing him to stagger backwards. Captain Hatfield was still on his feet and Cargalis walked calmly up to him and stabbed him in the forehead and then in the side. Captain Hatfield fell but he was still breathing. Richard MacDonald, who was on the bridge, rushed towards the captain and began to drag him along the deck in an attempt to take him below. Yet, Caludis attacked the second mate and stabbed him twice. He staggered towards Kenesa, pleading for his life, but he shoved the wounded man away, after which Caludis stabbed him three times in the neck.

By this time, Joseph Wortley realised his life was in danger and climbed up into the rigging. Cacaris was now in possession of a revolver and fired at the chief mate three times but failed to hit him. At this point, Petersen and Renken fled into a cabin as they feared for their lives despite having been assured by Cargalis that they would not be harmed as it was only the officers he and his compatriots wished to kill. Twenty minutes later, Kaida fired again up into the rigging and now badly wounded, the chief mate fell to the deck where he was stabbed by Cacaris. As he lay struggling for breath, Cargalis knelt on his chest and finished him off by cutting his throat with such savagery that he almost decapitated him. The mutineers had achieved their aims and the bodies of the three officers were thrown overboard.

Lettis discounted any suggestion that the crimes were committed because of the cruelty of the officers, which might have led the killers to believe their lives were threatened. It appeared to have been carefully planned and this was subsequently confirmed by Kenesa in a conversation the pair had as they were being held in France, awaiting deportation to England. The Greek repeated what he had told Von Hoydonck about their intentions and added that he and his countrymen had begun planning the crime almost from the moment they had first met in London.

When the *Lennie*'s small boat carrying the six fugitives came ashore at Les Sables d'Olonne, they informed the Commissary of Marine that they were the surviving crewmembers of the Greek brigantine *St Georges* that was carrying a cargo of wheat from Constantinople to Le Havre, which had sunk. Nonetheless, the commissary had been advised of the murders on the *Lennie* by telegraph and was aware of the true identities of the six men who were taken into custody.

Arrangements were made for all the survivors to return to England and they were accompanied on the journey by a team of officers from Scotland Yard under the command of Superintendent Frederick Williamson. It was decided subsequently that the following were to be charged with the one count of murdering Captain Hatfield: Cargalis, Moros, Leosis, Kenesa, Cacaris, Kaida, Caludis, Angelos and Renken. At the beginning of April 1876, they appeared before Sir Thomas Henry at Bow Street Magistrates Court. After the crown case was presented, Henry agreed with those representing Moros that there was no evidence against him and he was discharged and released. The remaining eight prisoners were committed to stand trial at the Old Bailey.

Meanwhile, decomposing body parts began to be washed up on beaches near Rochefort and these consisted of three heads and a headless torso. In order to preserve them until the English police could inspect the mutilated body parts, they were buried in the sand close to where they were found. Superintendent Williamson and Von Hoydonck made the journey across the Channel but by the time they arrived, the weather had been particularly poor and the heads had been washed out to sea. The torso, however, was recovered and sixteen knife wounds were discovered. As the deceased had clearly been a tall man, it was thought to be the body of Captain Hatfield. Unfortunately, the hand on which he had a distinguishing tattoo was so badly decomposed that it was impossible to make a definite identification and the torso could not therefore be used as evidence by the crown lawyers.

At the trial, the jury accepted the claims of Leosis, Renken, Kenesa and Angelos that they had been coerced into participating in the mutiny and played relatively minor roles. They had grounds for believing their lives would have been put in jeopardy had they not done so and were found not guilty. Nevertheless, compelling evidence was provided by the testimonies of Von Hoydonck (who was rewarded with fifty pounds from public funds for his bravery), Troussilot, Lettis and Petersen, which led to Cacaris, Cargalis, Caludis and Kaida being convicted and sentenced to death. They were executed at eight o'clock on the morning of 23 May 1876 by William Marwood in Newgate Prison. Among the small group of spectators allowed to witness the event was the Greek Consul, Mr G. P. Lascardi, and the condemned men were accompanied on the scaffold by Dr Hieronymus Myriantheus, the Archimandrite at the Greek Church in London.

9

The *Rising Sun*, 1881

The fishing smack *Rising Sun* sailed out of Albert Dock at Hull, heading for the fishing grounds of the North Sea on the morning of 16 December 1881. She was part owned and skippered by twenty-seven-year-old Oswald Otto Brand who had been at sea since his youth and was therefore an experienced sailor and fisherman. He had a crew of five, of which the two most experienced were John Dench, the second hand, and the third hand was Frederick Rycroft. In addition, there were two fisherboys, William Blackburn and David Yates. The youngest member of the crew was fourteen-year-old William Papper who eight months earlier had been apprenticed to Brand for seven years by his parents. William was an 'indoor apprentice', meaning that when not at sea, he lived with Brand and his wife in their home. At sea, he undertook a wide range of duties including those of cook.

The crew had joined the boat on the night of 15 December and as young William went aboard, Brand was saying farewell to his wife on the dockside. As he passed, the youngster was heard to say, 'My sister knows you, skipper.' Brand asked, 'Who is your sister?' William replied, 'Emma Papper of Trundle Street.' This was in a notorious district of Hull in which a number of brothels were located and Brand seemed a little taken aback and embarrassed but said nothing further.

The *Rising Sun* was at sea for almost three weeks and returned to port on 5 January 1882. Brand, accompanied by Rycroft, Dench and Blackburn, visited William's parents to give them the sad news that on New Year's Day, their son was lost overboard in a fierce storm 120 miles off Spurn Point. A high wind caught the large foresail sheet that carried him over the side and despite a thorough search of the area they could not find him. Mr and Mrs Papper were extremely distressed on hearing the news but were also unhappy with the explanation given by Brand.

They suspected that William might have been the victim of foul play as they knew from their son and others that Brand would at times ill-treat his crews. They made their concerns known to Brand who turned to the other crewmembers, all of whom supported their skipper's version of events. William's parents had little option other than to accept this account and his death was reported to the local police and the Shipping Office, enabling William's mother and father to make a claim for compensation.

Sadly, such accidents were far from unusual. Between January 1878 and December 1881, twenty-eight adults and fifty-nine youths and apprentices had been lost at sea from Hull fishing smacks. There were considered to be no grounds for any further investigations on this occasion and William was simply recorded as being the first loss of 1882. In the weeks that followed, the *Rising Sun,* skippered by Brand and with the same crew, made two further voyages into the North Sea.

However, on 1 March, there was a dramatic development. Dench, Blackburn and Yates made statements to Hull's Chief Constable, James Campbell, in which they claimed that William Papper did not die accidentally, but was murdered by Brand and that Rycroft had also played a major role in his death. Both men were subsequently arrested and when charged with the wilful murder of the youngster, Brand told the chief constable, 'It's false. There's others in it besides me.' The three accusers admitted in their statements they had each thrown ice cold water over William as he was standing naked on the deck in freezing weather. Still, they only did so under protest and because they feared what Brand might do to them if they disobeyed his order. He was known to carry a loaded revolver with him when at sea and Dench told of an earlier incident on another smack, the *Dream*, when he shot at a deckhand, narrowly missing his head. The three *Rising Sun* crewmembers insisted he fired it menacingly a number of times on the return journey to Hull following William's death and these were taken to be warnings that none of them should contact the police, for if they did there would be dire consequences.

Brand and Rycroft made several appearances before a packed Hull police court. On one of these, Dench walked close to the dock and Brand had to be restrained by the police officer who was escorting him. Brand screamed, 'Take that bastard away if you want me to keep quiet.' Feelings were running high and at the close of each hearing, as the prisoners were being taken down into the cells, they were loudly hissed and booed by those in the public gallery. Therefore, it came as no surprise that once they had been committed to stand trial, it was decided to hear the case away from Hull, given the difficulty in finding jury members in the district who would not be hostile towards the accused men before any evidence was heard.

The trial opened on 4 May at the Yorkshire Spring Assizes held in Leeds Town Hall before Mr Justice Watkin Williams. It lasted two days and part-way through, the crown acknowledged that having listened to the testimony of its own witnesses, there was insufficient evidence to convict Rycroft of murder. He was believed to have acted out of fear of Brand as it was accepted he had fired his revolver at him throughout the voyage to enforce obedience and to intimidate him. Furthermore, Rycroft had been heard to plead with Brand to spare the lad from some of the worst violence meted out to him. Rycroft was therefore convicted of the less serious offences of common assault and inflicting grievous bodily harm and was sentenced to three months' imprisonment with hard labour. This left Brand standing alone in the dock and those in their mid-thirties and older, on hearing the account of brutality and abuse that was given, must have recalled the case of Captain Rogers a quarter of a century earlier.

Dench told the court that after his wife had left the dockside on the night before setting sail, Brand came aboard and said to him that William Papper would pay for telling lies about an illicit relationship with his sister in front of his wife. Later that night when Brand confronted the youngster with the accusation, William denied having done so, but Brand could not be persuaded otherwise and was clearly intent on making the boy pay dearly. On the first night at sea, Brand cast anchor off Sunk Island. All of the crew were on deck and Brand ordered William below, supposedly on an errand. However, he followed the lad and seconds later Brand was heard to shout, 'I have done for your sister, now I will do for you. Now you bugger, I will learn you to tell tales.' William returned on deck five minutes later, his face swollen and bleeding. This would prove to be the first of almost daily beatings and other forms of ill-treatment, the brutality of which intensified as the days passed.

On 23 December, the *Rising Sun* was at Dogger Bank when without warning or provocation, Brand knocked William to the deck and ordered the crew to pour buckets of cold water over him. The weather was freezing and William was told he could not change out of his soaking clothes and was ordered to repeat out loud, 'If I had not been a bad lad, I would not be here.' He was forced to spend the next seven days and nights on deck, exposed to the appalling winter weather as the smack struggled against rough seas and high winds. On another occasion, a rope was tied around the lad's neck and arms and he was dragged along the deck by Brand who was shouting, 'I'll hang him!' The rope was thrown over the crosstrees and the skipper ordered Blackburn to operate the winch to haul him up. At first, Blackburn refused to obey the order but eventually did so, following threats uttered by Brand. William was lifted four to five feet off the deck and Brand grabbed his legs to pull him downwards. William would almost certainly have died had the crosstrees not broken, which resulted in him falling and as he lay struggling for breath, Brand kicked him repeatedly.

On Christmas Day, while his shipmates were eating a dinner of roast duck and plum pudding, William was again forced to remain on deck. At the end of the meal, bones and other leftovers were fed to the skipper's dog and it was only after he had finished that the scraps were handed to William. He begged Brand for a biscuit, a plea that was ignored although later, the crew gave him a little food and water without the captain's knowledge. As usual, Boxing Day began with a severe beating for William, but Brand had devised a new form of torture. A heavy weight was tied to the end of a rope, the other end of which was given to William. The weight was thrown into the rough seas and he was ordered to pull it back on board. Surprisingly, he managed to do so, which led Brand to tie a much heavier weight to the end of the rope that once more was thrown into the sea. This time, William could not complete the task and was close to collapse. Brand went below for a few minutes allowing Dench to step forward and pull the weight on to the boat and the others agreed to inform Brand that William had completed the task unaided.

The next day was the youngster's fourth day exposed to the elements and he pleaded with Brand to be allowed to change into dry clothes. At first, it seemed that Brand was prepared to agree to the request but this proved not to be the case. He ordered the crew to strip him naked and throw him into the tub in which the fish were kept. When finally allowed out, he was not permitted to dry himself with a towel, but was forced to run up and down the deck.

On the morning of the twenty-ninth, William was allowed to eat a dumpling, but this was not a sign that Brand's attitude towards him had mellowed as would become evident later that day. There was no proper water closet on the smack and William went below to relieve himself in the bucket used for that purpose; however, he had not sought permission and when advised by Rycroft what he had done, Brand flew into a rage.

He ordered the lad to be dragged back, together with the bucket. Using a long brush, Brand picked up the excrement and daubed it over William. He was then tied to the ship's rail and Dench and Blackburn were once again ordered to throw buckets of cold water over him. William was too weak to cry out and Brand screamed prophetically, 'Say your prayers as you won't live another day on this boat.' Indeed, William's torment was almost at an end.

The dill was the foulest place on the boat as it contained a large amount of sewage, bilge water and other filth and was situated at the very bottom of the vessel. Brand gave the order for its cover to be removed and for William, who could offer no resistance, to be lowered into it. Dench pleaded on the lad's behalf but Brand would not listen and stood on William's shoulders, ensuring he was almost totally immersed in the dill's disgusting contents. When he was at last pulled out, the crew heard him whisper 'God help me.' There was to be no help and as he lay on the deck unable to defend himself, Brand beat him with a stick. When Dench told him that the boy was dying, the skipper replied, 'A good thing too,' before going below.

Later, Brand agreed that an attempt to revive William could be made, but decided that this should be done by instilling a sense of fear in him. He ordered that William be wrapped in a canvas with only his head showing and dangled over the side close to the surface of the sea. This failed and he was hauled back aboard. He was a pitiful sight, covered in bruises and cuts and his face was so horribly disfigured and swollen that he was unrecognisable. He died at six o'clock and Brand must have known that if the corpse was returned to Hull, foul play would almost certainly be suspected. He therefore concocted a tale to cover up the events leading to William's death, but realised that Yates would not agree to such a scheme. However, he secured the agreement of Dench, Rycroft and Blackburn who colluded for a number of reasons. First, they were in fear of Brand; second, each relied on him for their livelihood; and third, they feared being implicated in William's death.

The corpse was hidden from Yates until the early hours of the following morning when Rycroft was on watch. The body was then thrown over the side and Rycroft raised a false alarm that William had been swept into the sea. The boat was stopped and a fruitless search of the area supposedly made. Also, it was agreed that Brand would report that the death occurred on New Year's Day and the three crewmembers would accompany him to the home of Mr and Mrs Papper to support his account as Brand realised William's parents might not believe him.

The crown's case was that the accused murdered his apprentice because of a perceived accusation made regarding his relationship with his victim's sister. Death had not resulted from a single act of violence when in a rage, but was due to a prolonged course of persistent and sadistic cruelty. For the defence, there was no crewmember to call upon to provide an alternative version of events and an attempt was therefore made to destroy the credibility of the prosecution witnesses and demonstrate that Brand was the victim of a conspiracy of lies.

There was said to have been no gun on board the boat on the fateful voyage and this had been made up by the crown witnesses. It was suggested to the jury that if the crew feared Brand as much as they claimed, they would not have sailed with him as frequently as they had in the past. His barrister described the huge responsibility that rested on the shoulders of a captain at sea, pointing out that it was no easy task to ensure the well-being of the crew and the sea-worthiness of his vessel. It was sometimes necessary for extreme measures to be used against disobedient, lazy or negligent seamen, which to those with no knowledge of the sea and its traditions will appear to be unduly harsh. It was not uncommon for beatings to be administered with fists and ropes and food to be withdrawn for the purpose of maintaining good order. Furthermore, it was said that with the possible exception of Yates, the other crown witnesses had participated willingly in the punishments which were meted out to William. If the jury believed the dead youth suffered acts of violence, they had to be seen within their proper context. If it was thought Brand had acted alone it should be acknowledged that the violence was not done with any malicious intent and he should be found innocent of any crime.

The jury was absent for ten minutes before returning with a guilty verdict of wilful murder. Sentencing him to death, the judge declared that given the evidence, no other verdict was possible and added, 'I have never known a crime of greater atrocity than that which the jury has convicted you of.' Told he would hang, Brand was removed from the dock and led to the cells below to the sound of loud cheering that greeted the death sentence. This reflected the widespread contempt in which he was held and no petition was raised to try and save him from the gallows. Resigned to his fate and following his final meeting with his wife, the condemned man wrote a letter, which the governor of the gaol promised to deliver to the Home Secretary after the execution.

He opened the document by emphasising that he did not have a revolver in his possession on the *Rising Sun* as the crown witnesses had claimed; however, he acknowledged that he struck William during the first two days of the voyage for minor breaches of discipline and afterwards, his behaviour and attitude improved so the beatings stopped. This, he insisted, was a common method of maintaining discipline on fishing smacks and most of their skippers resorted to such methods on a regular basis. William's behaviour worsened after Christmas Eve and although he denied withdrawing food at any time, he did order buckets of water to be thrown over him and he did indeed say he would hang him, but this was an empty threat that he had no intention of carrying out.

He named Dench and Blackburn as the murderers for they had been responsible for most of the violence and it was they who had beaten William incessantly, forced excrement into his mouth and pushed him into the dill. When the lad died, he and Rycroft decided initially that the body would have to be taken back to Hull. Nonetheless, they reluctantly agreed to throw it into the sea having been begged to do so by Dench and Blackburn who feared being accused of murder. He concluded by reminding the Home Secretary that in the previous seven years, he had nine apprentices and there had not been one complaint about his behaviour towards any of them.

Indeed, there was a widely-held belief in Hull that most of the other crewmembers bore some responsibility for allowing the crime to occur and this became evident at the conclusion of the trial. Dench was attacked in his lodgings at Leeds and his three assailants were believed to be Hull fishermen who sought to inflict punishment on him. However, only Brand faced the noose for William's murder. On the morning of 2 May, shortly before eight o'clock in the morning, a small group of journalists gathered at the gallows that had been erected in the exercise yard adjoining Armley's B Wing. They watched Brand climb the steps and stand on the drop where the hangman, William Marwood, was waiting for him. A few minutes later, the prison's black flag was hoisted to signify the murderer was dead.

By this time, the *Rising Sun* had been sold to new owners, its name changed and once more it was in the fishing grounds of the North Sea.

10

The *Melrose Castle*, 1883

Shortly before midnight on 6 May 1882, the Prime Minister, William Ewart Gladstone and his wife, accompanied by the Marquis of Hartington and Lady Louisa Egerton, arrived unexpectedly at the home of Lord and Lady Cavendish in London's Carlton House Terrace. The premier and Mrs Gladstone were extremely distressed and asked to speak to their niece, Lady Cavendish. The Gladstones were the bearers of tragic news for five hours earlier at a few minutes past seven, their niece's husband, Lord Frederick Cavendish, the newly appointed Chief Secretary for Ireland, had been assassinated in Dublin. Murdered at his side was the most senior civil servant in Ireland, Thomas Henry Burke, the Permanent Undersecretary.

Lord Cavendish had arrived in Dublin that very morning and a few hours later was sworn in at a ceremony attended by Mr Burke who read out the Queen's Letters Patent. Later, as it was a pleasant evening, Lord Cavendish decided to walk along the public footpath that passed through Phoenix Park and led to the Chief Secretary's Lodge, his new home. This stood close to the official residence of the Permanent Undersecretary and as usual Mr Burke had taken a cab home, but on passing Cavendish, alighted with the intention of walking with him. However, the two men would never reach their residences, for as they walked through the park, they were attacked by a group of men who stabbed them both to death. No witnesses came forward but an examination of the scene revealed that several men must have been involved and they had taken only a few minutes to carry out the killings. The bodies were taken to the nearby Madame Steevens' Hospital where post-mortems were performed. Fifty-three-year-old Burke had suffered a massive wound to his chest and a knife had been driven with such force into his throat in an upwards direction that several teeth were dislodged. There was a third wound to his face and others to his arms and hands, sustained as he tried to defend himself. Cavendish was forty-six years of age and a knife was plunged into his chest with sufficient force to penetrate his lungs and his arms bore several defensive wounds. The two unarmed men stood no chance against a group of such determined killers who had struck so horrifically at the heart of the British establishment.

The task of capturing the assassins was given to Superintendent Joseph Mallon of the Dublin Metropolitan Police. Within days, he came to realise that those responsible were not American sympathisers of the republican movement as was first thought by many, but were members of the recently formed Irish National Invincibles. This was a brutal splinter group of the Irish Republican Brotherhood that was determined to murder British civil servants, leading politicians and members of the judiciary and juries responsible for convicting supporters of Irish republicanism. It was learnt later that they planned to kill only Burke and it was Cavendish's misfortune to have been walking at his side at the time of the attack.

In the weeks that followed, there were a number of arrests and in early 1883, more than twenty men suspected of being Invincibles and of conspiracy to murder appeared in court for preliminary proceedings. The suspects were held in Kilmainham Prison and among them, to the surprise of many, was thirty-seven-year-old James Carey who was regarded as one of Dublin's leading and most respectable citizens. He began his working life as a bricklayer but in his early thirties founded his own hugely successful building company that had won many major government contracts. Carey played a leading role in Dublin's religious and social life and had a reputation for taking a keen interest in the welfare of the city's working class. He had always claimed to be apolitical and was elected to Dublin's council in 1882. Carey seemed destined to become the city's lord mayor in the not too distant future; however, his arrest on suspicion of being involved in the Phoenix Park assassinations exposed his hitherto strong republican sympathies for he had joined the Fenians as far back as 1861 and in 1881 became one of the leaders of the Invincibles.

One of the other arrested men, Michael Kavanagh, who under interrogation admitted taking several of the assassins to Phoenix Park in his cab, was persuaded to turn Queen's Evidence. He confirmed Carey was present when the men were stabbed and had given the signal for the attack to begin. Michael Flynn, an innocent builder who had recognised Carey and spoke to him, also placed him at the scene a few minutes

Two engravings of Portsmouth Harbour out of which the *Adventurer* sailed in September 1811. (*Both after paintings by Clarkson F. Stanfield, Publisher's collection*)

Marshalsea Prison where those hanged at Execution Dock spent their final hours. *Left*, and engraving from the late eighteenth century showing the courtyard; *below*, a photograph from the mid nineteenth century showing the external walls. Little would have been different from the time that Palm and Telling were there.

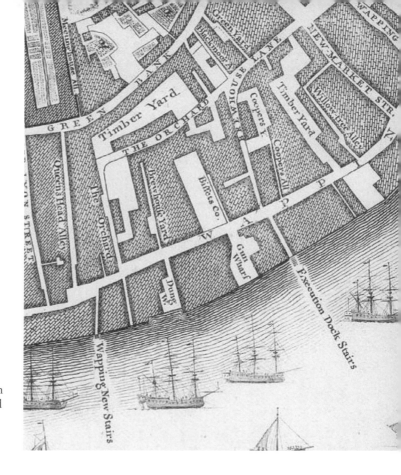

Right: Execution Dock. (*Author's collection*)

Below: The execution of Lieutenant Richard Stewart Gamage RN. (*Welcome Library, London*)

THE

TRIAL

OF

PETER HEAMAN

AND

FRANCOIS GAUTIEZ,

BEFORE THE

High Court of Admiralty,

AT EDINBURGH,

ON THE 26TH OF NOVEMBER, 1821,

FOR

PIRACY AND MURDER.

LEITH:

PRINTED AT THE COMMERCIAL LIST OFFICE, FOR WILLIAM
REID, BOOKSELLER, NO. 40, SHORE ; AND SOLD
BY ALL BOOKSELLERS.

1821.

Left: The transcript of the trial of Haemen and Gautiez that was sold in large numbers. (*Author's collection*)

Below: Calton Prison in which the condemned men spent their final hours. (*An engraving from a drawing by Thomas Hosmer Shepherd, Publisher's collection*)

Liverpool, c. 1832, with the Custom House on the left and the Canning Dock in the foreground. (*Publisher's collection*)

The Old Bailey in the early years of the 19th century. (*Author's collection*)

Slaves shipped across the South Atlantic to Brazil were kept in appalling conditions. (*Author's collection*)

Left: Lieutenant R. D. Stupart RN of HMS *Wasp. Centre:* Captain Joaquim Antonio de Cuquribio of the *Felicidade. Right:* Janus Majaval. (*Woolmer's Exeter and Plymouth Gazette*)

Above: Kirkdale House of Correction. (*Author's collection*)

Right: Thomas Wright, the prison philanthropist. (*National Portrait Gallery, London*)

William
Calcraft, the
hangman.
(*The
Illustrated
Police News*)

William
Marwood,
the hangman.
(*The
Illustrated
Police News*)

Above: Newgate Prison.
(*Publisher's collection*)

Right: The execution of
the *Lennie* mutineers. (*The
Illustrated Police News*)

The *Rising Sun*. (*Hull Museums*)

Oswald Otto Brand and other crew members. (*The Illustrated Police News*)

Right: James Carey. (*Author's collection*)

Below: There is uproar in the court when it becomes known that Carey is to testify against his former comrades. (*The Graphic*)

Patrick O'Donnell. (*Author's collection*)

An apologist *In Memoriam* Irish Nationalist sheet published in the USA. (*Publisher's collection*)

Richard Parker is killed by his skipper. (*The Illustrated Police News*)

As details of the tragedy emerged, there was a great deal of public sympathy for Thomas Dudley and his crew. (*The Illustrated Police News*)

Grimsby's wealth was based on fish. (*Author's collection*)

Above left: The murder of William Connolly. (*The Illustrated Police News*)

Above right: Gustav Rau. (*Author's collection*)

Moses Thomas (second from the left) poses in the courtroom with a model of the *Veronica*. (*Liverpool Records Office*)

Walton Prison. (*Author's collection*)

Left: Eileen Gibson. *Right:* James Camb. (*Author's collection*)

The *Durban Castle*. (*Author's collection*)

before the killings took place. As the preliminary hearings progressed, it was becoming evident to most observers that Carey played a significant role in the conspiracy and despite his confident demeanour, he would have great difficulty in persuading a jury of his innocence at a subsequent trial.

On the morning of 16 February, Carey was not in his usual seat in the dock with his comrades. There was a good deal of murmuring in the court, which turned to uproar when he entered through another door and sat in the witness box for he had agreed to become a crown witness in order to save his own neck. He began by confirming his membership of the Invincibles, told of his leading role in planning the assassination of Mr Burke and furthermore, that he was present when he and Lord Cavendish met their deaths. However, he was prepared to do more than confess to his own involvement, for his greatest act of betrayal as far as the republican movement was concerned, was to name the seven men who committed the murders and these were Joseph Brady, Timothy Kelly, Pat Delany, Thomas Caffrey, Michael Fagan, Daniel Curley and Joseph Hanlon. Carey's evidence was crucial at the subsequent trials of the accused as it led to the convictions and executions of five of them in Kilmainham Prison on five separate days in May and June 1883, all at the hands of hangman, William Marwood.

The first execution, which took place on 14 May, was that of twenty-two-year-old Joseph Brady who received his last visit from family members two days earlier. Among them was his mother who when questioned outside the prison gates described the great pride she felt for her son. She told reporters she would have disowned him if he had co-operated with the authorities by informing on others to save himself. Ten thousand supporters gathered outside the prison on the morning of the execution and there were many troops present, but there was no serious unrest.

Daniel Curley was hanged four days later and among the crowd at the gates of the prison was his father, who on seeing the black flag hoisted, indicating his son was dead, fell to his knees and wept. Curley's wife owned a confectioner's shop on Thomas Street, which had remained open for business until the previous day. However, it was now closed and attached to the door was a black bow and a card on which was written 'Daniel Curley, died 18th May 1883, aged 31 years. Rest in Peace'.

Twenty-four-year-old Michael Fagan's execution followed on 28 May and his brother was standing in the crowd. One hundred troops guarded the prison gates but again there were no problems. As the black flag was being raised, a woman fell to her knees cursing James Carey for his treachery and the cry was taken up by many others. Thomas Caffrey, who had once worked for Carey, was twenty-four years old when he was executed on 2 June. One week later, the final execution took place, which was that of Thomas Kelly, a youth whose date of birth was not known. He was thought to be nineteen years old and it was believed by many that he would be reprieved and a petition presented to the Home Secretary included the signatures of two members of the jury who had convicted him. In the hours before he died, Kelly was attended by a group of nuns and among them was the cousin of Thomas Burke.

Meanwhile, Carey remained in Kilmainham Prison, now reviled by the republican movement and many others less committed to the cause. He had been spared the noose and promised his freedom, but his hopes of a substantial financial reward and a pardon came to nought. Furthermore, he was advised that he and his family would not receive any protection on his release. He was given a stark choice: either walk out of prison and face certain death at the hands of his once republican friends or travel overseas with his wife and seven children under an assumed name, their fares being paid by the government. Despite an initial display of bravado, he opted unsurprisingly for the latter option. Fenians throughout the English-speaking world were asked to look out for Carey and his family, who were rumoured to be on their way to Bermuda or Canada, so the executed men could be avenged by his death.

It did not take long to find him for towards the end of July, it was reported from South Africa that Carey had been shot to death on board a passenger liner. There was an immediate outburst of rejoicing throughout Ireland with bonfires being lit and his effigy burnt in many districts of Dublin. Six fires were lit in Denzil Street where Carey had lived and it proved impossible for the police to extinguish them because of the large number of republican sympathisers who had gathered there to celebrate.

It was later revealed that on 1 July, tickets were booked in the Dublin office of Donald Currie & Co. for a Mr and Mrs Power and their seven children to travel to South Africa on the *Kinfauns Castle,* which was due to sail from London three days later. It is highly probable that any republican being made aware of this would immediately suspect, correctly, the tickets were for the Carey family and this would allow sufficient time to make arrangements for a ticket to be obtained for an assassin to join the ship. Mrs Carey, whose maiden name was Power, sailed with the children from London and her husband boarded the ship at Dartmouth. During the voyage, Carey was a regular visitor to the bar and circulated freely among the other passengers. He became particularly friendly with a man named Patrick O'Donnell who was travelling with a young woman and the two men were often seen playing cards together. On arrival at Cape Town, Carey and his family transferred to the *Melrose Castle* that was to take them to Natal. O'Donnell and his woman friend also boarded the vessel, which was built in Glasgow in 1877, specifically to carry passengers along the South African coast.

On 29 July, as the ship sailed between Table Bay and Algoa Bay, the two men were sitting together in the second-class lounge, apparently still on very good terms; however, O'Donnell suddenly pulled a revolver from his pocket and taking deliberate aim, shot Carey in the neck. The wounded man struggled to his feet and attempted to reach his wife who was standing nearby. As he did so, there was a second shot that hit Carey in the back. He stumbled into his wife's arms and cried out, 'Maggie, I am shot! O'Donnell has shot me!' Another bullet was fired into his back and he fell to the floor. Mrs Carey screamed at O'Donnell, accusing him of murdering her husband, to which O'Donnell replied that he knew her real surname was Carey and the true identity of her husband, adding, 'I was sent to do it.' Carey died twenty minutes later. The gunman was detained by the crew and taken to Port Elizabeth where he was arrested and charged with Carey's murder.

The forty-five-year-old suspect was born in Gweedore, County Donegal, and had been an active republican since 1864. During the Fenian Rising of 1867, O'Donnell played a leading role in what became known as the Battle of Tallaght and afterwards escaped to England where he lived in Preston for some time. In 1871, O'Donnell emigrated to California where he worked as a miner for several years but retained his links to the Fenian movement. In 1882, now living in New York, it was believed that he was sent to Dublin following the Phoenix Park murders to monitor events on behalf of supporters of Irish republicanism in America and to offer financial support to the men charged with the killings.

Enquiries revealed that on the eve of the departure of the *Kinfauns Castle*, O'Donnell was in London and bought tickets for the young woman and himself for their journey to Natal (she did not subsequently face any criminal charges). On his last night in England, he told a group of friends that he was travelling to South Africa on a mission of great importance but refused to elaborate further. O'Donnell returned to England and his trial opened on 30 November 1883 at the Old Bailey before Mr Justice Denman. In the dock, O'Donnell chewed on tobacco in what the press described as the 'American way' and occasionally would spit on the floor to show his contempt for the prosecution witnesses and the evidence they were giving. He had pleaded not guilty and denied being sent by an organisation on a mission to assassinate Carey. The crown opted not to attempt to prove otherwise and it has never been established if he was or was not aware of Carey's true identity when the *Kinfauns Castle* sailed out of London.

Robert Cubitt, a Norfolk ironmonger who was a passenger on the *Kinfauns Castle* with his brother Frank, was in a Cape Town bar on the evening of 28 July as passengers waited to continue their journey on the *Melrose Castle*. Also present was O'Donnell and the landlord showed them both a newspaper that contained a sketch of Carey. It was immediately obvious that it was in fact their fellow passenger, Mr Power, and the witness heard the accused, who seemed surprised at the revelation, respond by saying, 'I'll shoot him.'

Three witnesses were called who saw the shooting, two of whom were members of the crew, namely James Parish, a steward, and the boatswain, Thomas Jones. The third was fifteen-year-old Thomas Carey, the son of the dead man, who was sitting close to his father when the first shot was fired. Thomas confirmed that his father was given a gun by the authorities in Dublin to offer him some protection, but at the time he was shot he was not carrying it.

O'Donnell insisted he had not known that Carey was his travelling companion until he saw his likeness in the Cape Town bar. After doing so, he decided to confront him but not to kill him. O'Donnell claimed to have shot Carey in self-defence for when he shouted 'I want nothing to do with you. You are James Carey, the bloody Irish informer,' Carey pulled a revolver from his pocket, but O'Donnell was able to shoot first. Walter Young, a cabman, was called as a defence witness. He had been responsible for driving Mrs Carey and her children, including Thomas, during the proceedings in South Africa. He testified that Thomas had told him on more than one occasion that his father had a revolver in his pocket at the time of the shooting. When he addressed the jury, O'Donnell's barrister argued that if his client had intended to murder Carey, he would not have done so in a room in which there were several witnesses at four-thirty in the afternoon. Rather, he would have waited until the two of them were alone and at night.

The jury retired for two hours and during that time they returned to seek guidance from the judge on two occasions. This led O'Donnell and his lawyers to believe there would be a not guilty verdict; however, they were mistaken and he was convicted of the murder. As the judge was passing the sentence of death, O'Donnell shouted, 'Three cheers for Old Ireland. Down with Queen Victoria,' before he was subdued and taken to the cells below. Most of the support for a reprieve came from abroad, especially America. The French novelist Victor Hugo also pleaded for O'Donnell's life and in a letter to the Queen, he wrote the following: 'The Queen of England has shown more than once her greatness of heart. The Queen of England will grant the condemned man O'Donnell his life and will accept the profound thanks of the civilised world.' Still, there was no reprieve and O'Donnell was executed in Newgate Prison by Bartholomew Binns on the morning of 17 December. He made no statement on the scaffold and died bravely.

He was buried within the walls of the prison, but some weeks later, a large crowd assembled at the O'Donnell family grave in Derrybeg in the parish of Gweedore and buried a coffin on which a plate was fastened bearing the inscription 'Sacred to the memory of Patrick O'Donnell, executed in London, December 17th, 1883'. Resolutions were passed, thanking supporters in America and Victor Hugo for attempting to save his life.

As for the *Melrose Castle*, she was later sold to an English company, renamed *Annie Hough* and was used on the Liverpool–Falmouth–London service. In 1901, she was sold to a French company and renamed *Emyre* and in 1905, was purchased by a company in Madagascar where she was wrecked in 1911.

11

The *Mignonette*, 1884

In early 1884, Jack Want, a wealthy Australian barrister, purchased the yawl *Mignonette*, fifty-two feet in length and weighing thirty-three tons, which had been built in Brightlingsea, Essex, seventeen years earlier. The new owner decided not to send it as cargo to his home in Sydney, but instead hired an English crew to sail her into the southern hemisphere. The vessel was refitted for the voyage and thirty-two-year-old Thomas Dudley agreed to be her captain.

Dudley was a hugely successful yachtsman who had won many prestigious racing prizes for the owners who employed him on a regular basis. Shortly before his appointment as captain of the *Mignonette*, he had acted as skipper of the steam yacht *Myrtle* for Sir Charles Strickland on a Mediterranean cruise. The father of three children, Dudley lived in Sutton, Surrey, where his wife taught in an infant school. Two years earlier, he entered into a business partnership and opened a greengrocer's shop as he wished to settle down and spend time with his young family. Unfortunately, the venture was unsuccessful and he returned to a life at sea.

Three other crewmembers were taken on for the journey. Thirty-seven-year-old Edwin Stephens of Southampton, a married man with five children, was engaged as mate and he had experience of a disaster at sea, having been chief officer on the steamer *European* that sank in the Bay of Biscay sometime earlier. Thirty-seven-year-old Edmund Brooks, who lived with his wife in Brightlingsea, was taken on to act as a rating. Richard Parker who was seventeen years of age, but claimed to be one year older, was chosen to be the cabin boy. A native of Southampton, he was an orphan whose only living relative was an older brother. Parker had been offered a similar position on another yacht, but opted to sail on the *Mignonette* as it provided him with the opportunity of travelling to Australia where he hoped to settle and start a new life. The *Mignonette* set sail from Fay's Yard in Southampton at five o'clock on the afternoon of 19 May 1884. Dudley opted for the longer South Atlantic route rather than sail through the Suez Canal as he believed the high winds often encountered in the Mediterranean might possibly put the boat at risk.

The first two weeks of the voyage passed uneventfully and on 1 June, the crew reached Madeira where they stayed overnight and took on water and provisions. On 14 June, Dudley and his crew were invited aboard the Liverpool ship *Bride of Horne* in mid-ocean. Captain Frazer took their letters, which he promised to post to their families on arrival in England so they would know they were safe. Three days later, the *Mignonette* crossed the equator and on 18 June, it sailed into appalling weather, which continued for many days. Despite the poor conditions, the crew faced no major problems until four o'clock on the afternoon of 5 July, by which time the boat was 1,600 miles from the nearest land. Stephens was steering and saw a massive wave heading towards them. There was time for him to shout a warning and Dudley, who was also on deck, was able to grab hold of the vessel's side. Everyone was safe but unfortunately many of the *Mignonette*'s timbers were loosened, smashed or washed away. Dudley realised immediately that the boat was doomed and gave the order for the dinghy, which was just thirteen-feet long, to be lowered into the water. Dudley made sure his shipmates were safe in the little boat before at great risk to himself, he went below to grab the sextant, compass and chronometer together with the emergency water supply. Unfortunately, most of the food and water was swept away and all that was saved were two tins of turnips, each of which contained five pieces.

Within five minutes of being struck by the wave, the *Mignonette* had disappeared beneath the waves. Fortunately, the instruments necessary for navigation were safe in the dinghy and the skipper knew these would be invaluable if they were to reach the major shipping lanes and stand any chance of being rescued. During their first night adrift, the men had to fight off a shark with an oar and this would prove to be only the start of their truly terrible ordeal. On the second day, they shared out some of the contents of one of the tins of turnips, which lasted for two days. On the fourth day, they came across a turtle that was pulled aboard and slaughtered. It provided each man with three pounds of meat, which had been consumed within one week, and afterwards they chewed on the bones and leathery skin. They also drank its blood as it rained only occasionally and for short periods. An attempt was made to store some of the turtle's blood in the casing of the chronometer, but it became contaminated with sea water and had to be discarded.

By this time, Dudley and his crew had been adrift for fourteen days and it became necessary to eat the remaining tin of turnips as it had proved impossible to catch any fish. Furthermore, in the absence of rainfall, the men had begun to drink their own urine and what was only now becoming evident was that Parker had been drinking large quantities of seawater, which was causing him to become seriously ill and delirious. On the fifteenth day and in an attempt to make better progress, Dudley made a makeshift sail out of their shirts and used an oar as a mast.

However, their predicament continued to worsen as they had been without food and water for several days. During this period, Parker continued to drink sea water and was in an even worse physical and mental state than previously. On the nineteenth day, Dudley believed desperate measures had to be taken. He proposed they draw lots to determine which of them should be killed so that the others might feed off the corpse, thus giving them a greater chance of survival. Parker was not capable of giving his views as he was insensible and Stephens was unsure. Brooks was opposed to the idea, saying it would be preferable they should all die together and Dudley did not press the matter any further that day. On the following day, Dudley proposed to Stephens and Brooks that rather than draw lots, they should simply kill Parker. He argued that unlike the others, the youngster had no wife or children and he was clearly close to death already. If he was sacrificed now, Dudley believed his body parts and blood would be more nutritious than if they waited for him to die. Stephens agreed, albeit reluctantly, but Brooks remained hostile to the plan. Dudley offered to slaughter the lad and Stephens agreed to hold him down should it become necessary to do so. Brooks refused to participate and with the agreement of his companions, went to the front of the dinghy where he covered his eyes with his hands, unable to watch what was about to take place.

Dudley spent a few moments in silent prayer before approaching Parker who was lying in the bottom of the boat. The youth was too weak to offer any resistance and it was not necessary for Stephens to pin him down. In a gentle voice, Dudley told him, 'Richard, your time has come.' Barely able to speak, the youngster asked, 'What? Me, sir?' 'Yes, my boy,' came the whispered reply as Dudley stabbed him in the neck with a small penknife and severed his jugular vein. Blood gushed from the open wound and was caught in the tins which had contained the turnips and navigation instruments. Over the next four days, all of the men, including Brooks, drank the blood and fed off the youth's heart and liver. That was until 29 July, the twenty-fourth day of their ordeal, when 900 or so miles from Rio de Janeiro and having drifted for 700 miles, the men saw a ship on the horizon. Fortunately, they had been spotted and the ship altered course to pick them up.

It was the German barque, *Montezuma*, under the command of Captain Simmonsen on her return voyage to Hamburg. Ninety minutes after first seeing the dinghy, the barque was alongside but only Brooks was able to climb aboard unaided. Dudley and Stephens were so weak they had to be carried by members of the German crew. The dinghy was taken aboard with Parker's mutilated remains still inside. It was obvious what had happened and this was confirmed by Dudley who gave a full account to Captain Simmonsen. Parker was wrapped in a shroud and buried at sea and as far as their hosts were concerned, the three Englishmen had done nothing wrong. They had simply acted in accordance with the customs of the sea and were treated as honoured guests for the month and a half they were on board.

The *Montezuma* entered Falmouth Harbour on 6 September and the three survivors were taken immediately to the customs house. The Merchant Shipping Acts required statements to be taken from the crew of any vessel lost at sea and they were met by Mr R. D. Cheeseman, the Receiver of Wrecks for East Cornwall. Thinking they had done nothing wrong, they gave full and truthful accounts of their adventures, including details of killing Parker and wilfully indulging in cannibalism. Having signed their statements, the men's thoughts turned to making arrangements for the journeys to their homes and families.

However, Sergeant of the Harbour Police James Lavery decided that the matter required further investigation. He telegraphed the Board of Trade and Home Office in London for guidance and persuaded the Mayor of Falmouth, Henry Liddicott, to issue warrants authorising the arrests of the three men who to their astonishment found themselves being taken to the local police cells. Held over the weekend, they were visited by an embarrassed mayor who apologised for any inconvenience caused and assured them they would be released by the town's magistrates on Monday morning.

What was not known to anyone in Falmouth was that high-level discussions were taking place in London, involving the Home Secretary, Sir William Harcourt, Sir Henry James, the Attorney General, and Sir

Farrer Herschel, the Solicitor General. There had been a great deal of publicity about the case and it was obvious that public opinion was very much on the side of the three survivors, but it was believed there were significant legal issues which needed to be addressed and it was decided the men should stand trial for murder. There was a sense of disbelief in Falmouth and beyond when on Monday morning the three men were remanded to the Borough Gaol until the following Thursday. By the time of their second appearance, Daniel Parker, brother of the dead youth, was present in the courtroom. He too was a sailor and a member of the crew of the yacht *Margaret* that was berthed in Torquay and her owner had granted him compassionate leave to attend the court hearing. There was a moving scene in the courtroom when Daniel approached the three accused men and shook each of them warmly by the hand.

Brooks never attempted to deny that he had fed off Parker's body, but Dudley and Stephens made it clear that he was against the actual killing and did not participate in it. The authorities therefore decided that Brooks should not be charged with any offence and would be asked to testify on behalf of the crown. The two others were charged with wilful murder and were committed to stand trial at Exeter Assizes but unusually for a capital case, they were granted bail. From the beginning, Brooks had insisted that the two defendants were decent and honourable men and Dudley was an excellent skipper to serve under. They had been forced to act as they did in order to survive.

When it became known the pair would have to stand trial, they received enormous support from the country's sailing fraternity and a defence fund was opened on their behalf. In a widely published letter seeking contributions, S. Herman Sturgis, Vice Commodore of the Corinthian Yacht Club, and Augustus G. Wildy, Rear Commodore of the Junior Thames Yacht Club, described the two accused as '...men of good character, who in their time had been foremost in the great national sport of yacht racing and were renowned for their pluck and zeal'.

The proceedings opened at Exeter Assizes on 3 November before trial judge Baron Huddleston and both defendants entered not guilty pleas. Arthur Charles QC prosecuted and Arthur Collins QC represented the accused. In the weeks following their safe return to England, public support for Dudley and Stephens had continued to grow and it was evident that the crown was aware of this. In opening the case, Charles acknowledged the men in the dock were essentially honourable men and the prosecution case was based solely on their own open and honest accounts of what happened in the dinghy. They had found themselves in an appalling predicament, but the killing of Parker was a premeditated act. The youngster posed no threat to either man, so the killing was therefore not done in self-defence and as lots were not drawn Parker could not be said to have been a willing participant.

On behalf of the accused men, Collins argued that they acted out of necessity and what they did was in accordance with the customs of the sea. This opinion was dismissed by Baron Huddleston who agreed with the crown that no such defence existed in case law. As the hearing progressed, Charles did not discount the possibility of clemency being shown to the two men, but that would be a matter to be decided following their convictions and in the meantime the members of the jury must act responsibly and convict them of murder. Nevertheless, the authorities, who were anxious to establish a legal precedent in this case, realised that no jury was likely to convict the men of a capital crime that might possibly lead to the gallows. It was widely believed at the time that Baron Huddleston was selected to act as the judge at their trial to prevent a sympathetic jury from refusing to convict.

Added weight to this theory came with the unusual decision he reached at the close of the evidence. The judge instructed the jury to return a special verdict, the first such conclusion to a trial since 1785. The jury was required to find the essential facts described by the crown to have taken place but not to deliver a verdict of guilt or innocence. This was done, but the members of the jury added that the accused men had their sympathy and they hoped the defendants would be shown mercy. Baron Huddleston declared that in his view the established facts were sufficient to convict the men of murder; however, it would be left to a higher court to formally agree to his findings and to sentence the men who were granted bail to appear at the Royal Courts of Justice in London later in the year. Dudley and Stephens duly appeared before Lord Chief Justice, Lord Coleridge, at a sitting of the Queen's Bench Division on 4 December. The idea of necessity as justification for their actions was rejected once again and Lord Coleridge posed two questions. First, who would decide what was necessary in any particular situation and second, on what grounds could the comparative values of lives be decided? He found the two men guilty of wilful murder and remanded them in custody for eight days when they would return to hear their sentences.

They were brought back to court on 12 December and before passing sentence, Lord Coleridge stated that he fully supported the Exeter jury's recommendation for mercy. He then sentenced Dudley and Stephens to death but broke with tradition by not placing the black cap on his head and concluded by adding 'And may the Lord have mercy on your souls.' Later that same day, they were reprieved and sentenced to six months' imprisonment. They were released from Holloway Prison on 20 May 1885.

By this time, Brooks had returned to the sea and Stephens is believed to have settled down to a life ashore with his family in Southampton. Dudley emigrated to Australia and opened a store in Sydney where he died of bubonic plague in 1900. A memorial tablet to Richard Parker was placed by the grave of his parents in a Southampton cemetery and at the request of his brother Daniel, the following words were added to the inscription:

Though he slay me, yet I will trust him. (Job xiii 15)
Lord, lay not this sin to their charge. (Acts xiii 60)

In 1838, forty-six years before Dudley and Stephens stood trial, Edgar Allan Poe published his novel *The Narrative of Arthur Gordon Pym of Nantucket*. In the book, the author's hero is involved in a number of adventures, in one of which he and three other men are adrift in a small boat. Driven by thirst and hunger, they decide to draw lots to choose who should be sacrificed so that the others might feed off his body and drink his blood to increase their chances of survival. The name of the man who was killed and eaten by the others was Richard Parker.

12

The *Doncaster*, 1889

Grimsby's importance and wealth grew in tandem with the expansion of its port, a process that began in the late 18th century. Goods arrived from across the globe and coal from the extensive mining areas of South Yorkshire was exported from there. However, it was the coming of the railway in the 1840s, resulting in easier access to London and in particular Billingsgate Fish Market, which led to the massive growth of the town's fishing fleet. The harbour was developed further with the opening of Number 1 Fish Dock in 1856 and a second in 1877. By the end of the 19th century, it was estimated that Grimsby was home to 500 or more fishing smacks, which sailed regularly into the dangerous waters of the North Sea.

One of those vessels was the *Doncaster*, owned by the Grimsby Ice Company, which sailed out of the port on 22 February 1889 under the command of forty-year-old William Connolly. His eighteen-year-old nephew, Walter Tennant Gempton, was taken on to act as cook for the voyage. The skipper lived with his wife and their two children on Kent Road in the town and the couple had known great tragedy as several of their children had died. Connolly served his apprenticeship on Hull boats, but for the previous twenty years had sailed out of Grimsby. He had an excellent reputation with the owners who employed him and with his crews. His nephew had a history of suffering from fits and was prone to outbursts of violence and on one such occasion in mid-1888, he made a determined attempt to strangle his mother. Gempton usually sailed with his father, but he had lost his boat which led to his uncle agreeing to take him on the *Doncaster* on a temporary basis and it was a decision that would cost the skipper his life.

On 6 March, a little over two weeks into the voyage, the *Doncaster* was fishing 240 miles east-north-east of Spurn. It was six o'clock in the evening and the captain was on deck, close to the companionway, talking to Arthur Turnell, one of the hands. Standing nearby was Henry Crow, another member of the crew, who would also witness the terrible events which occurred during the next fifteen minutes. Gempton had suffered from a fit two hours earlier and remained in an agitated state, pacing up and down the deck on the opposite side of the boat, talking to himself. Suddenly and without warning, he rushed across the deck and from behind, stabbed the captain in the neck with an open clasp knife. As he did so, the wounded man exclaimed, 'Oh, he has stabbed me.' His nephew fell upon him and screamed, 'You crafty bugger, has that settled you? That is a bit of Jack the Ripper. He wants to make off with the ship and all hands. He is Jack the Ripper.'

The stunned crew pulled Gempton off the captain who was carried to the bunk in his cabin. Despite his wound, the skipper was fully conscious and aware of what had happened to him. Turnell realised that the jugular vein was severed and a great deal of blood was being lost. He told Turnell, 'Put some flour on my neck. If you stop the blood I might live.' However, he could not be saved and died ten minutes later. Turnell returned on deck, grabbed hold of Gempton and said, 'Come down and look at the skipper now. He is dead.' In the cabin, there was no response from Gempton who simply stared at the corpse. He was locked in his cabin and the crew set a course for home.

The *Doncaster* sailed into Grimsby in the early hours of 14 March. The crew contacted Dock-Constable Lawton who boarded the vessel and was told of the tragedy. Arrangements were made for the corpse to be taken to Grimsby Hospital where a post-mortem confirmed how the captain had met his end. The constable took possession of the clasp knife and detained Gempton who was escorted to the police station on King Edward Street. Gempton was charged with murder and almost immediately he suffered from another fit. Dr Newby was called to the cells to treat him and Gempton was able to appear briefly before the local magistrates later that morning.

He was not the first prisoner to be called before the bench. William Chafer, a fisherman who had been arrested the previous night for being drunk and disorderly, was placed in the dock. Superintendent Waldran rose to his feet and addressed the court. Due to a lack of space, it had been necessary for Chafer to share a cell with Gempton who became increasingly distressed as the night progressed. Chafer did not go to sleep and was heard by several officers comforting the youth over a period of several hours and he had been a source of great support to him. Rather than being fined, he was thanked by the magistrates and allowed to leave without any penalty being imposed and with the appreciation of all those in the packed courtroom.

In the dock, Gempton was accompanied by his distraught mother throughout the hearing before being committed to stand trial in Lincoln to face the following charge that was read out by the clerk:

> On the information of Job Waldran, Head Constable, that he on the 11th March instant, on the high seas, while on a fishing voyage from Great Grimsby to the North Sea and back feloniously, wilfully and of his malice aforethought, did kill and murder William Connolly against the peace of our Sovereign Lady the Queen, her Crown and Majesty.

At an inquest held at the hospital, at which statements were given by Arthur Turnell and Henry Crow, the jury returned a verdict of wilful murder by Gempton. He was therefore also committed to the assizes on a coroner's warrant. In the days following Gempton's committal, it was learnt that his victim had written a letter to his wife while out at sea on the fatal voyage. He passed it over to the skipper of another Grimsby smack encountered in the North Sea that was heading home. Her skipper undertook to post it to Mrs Connolly on arrival in port. Part of it read:

> Walter has had no less than four fits since we came out, three in one day. Worse, you never know they are coming on. I have saved the bottle with hartshorn in for when Walter goes off and I clap it under his nose. He gets two or three good sniffs, it soon brings him to his feet but he is long kind of silly after.

The trial was due to open on 13 July before Mr Justice Hawkins at the County Hall, Lincoln, but the accused was not produced. The judge gave details of what he said was a motiveless crime, which the crown accepted was committed by a delusional youth who was suffering from serious mental health problems. Since appearing before the magistrates, Gempton had been found to be insane and unfit to stand trial and was confined in a lunatic asylum. Later, this tragic young man was transferred to Broadmoor Asylum for the criminally insane where it is reported he died four years later.

13

The *Veronica*, 1902

The *Veronica* was a British-owned barque, weighing approximately 1,060 tons, which set sail from Ship Island in Mississippi on 11 October 1902 with a cargo of timber destined for Montevideo. Her skipper was Captain Alexander Shaw, Alexander McLeod was the first mate and Fred Abrahamson the second mate, all of whom were British. There were two British deckhands, Julius Parsons and Patrick Doran, who, given his Irish roots, was also known as Paddy. There were six other hands: Swede Gustav Johansen, Indian Alexander Bravo, Willem Schmidt, a Dutchman, and three Germans, August Mailaha who was known as Gustav Rau, Otto Monson and Henry Flohr. Also on board was Moses Thomas, an American, who was the cook.

On 28 December, the *Brunswick*, under the command of Captain George Browne, was taking on its cargo at the island of Cajueira off the coast of Brazil in readiness for her return voyage to England. As he was supervising the work, the captain noticed a lifeboat bearing the name *Veronica* coming alongside. It contained five men and Rau introduced himself as the second mate. He explained that they were the only survivors of the ship's original crew and asked to be taken to England. The others in the boat were Schmidt, Monson, Flohr and Thomas.

Rau told Captain Browne of a voyage dogged by misfortune from the start. One of the crew, Johansen, was said to have died of fever as they sailed through the Straits of Florida and the first mate was reportedly killed when a topsail fell on him and he was swept overboard. To make matters worse, a fire broke out in the captain's cabin on 20 December that spread so rapidly through the wooden ship it was impossible to extinguish the flames. Captain Shaw gave the order to abandon ship and for the two lifeboats to be lowered into the sea. The captain and several other surviving crewmembers climbed into one, but it was swamped by a large wave almost immediately and all those in it were lost. Rau's boat drifted for five days and the five men survived on eleven biscuits and a small jug of fresh water they had managed to grab before taking to the lifeboat. They reached Cajueira on Christmas Day and were waiting for a boat to rescue them when the *Brunswick* arrived. Captain Browne had no reason to doubt this account and welcomed the men aboard, having agreed to take them back to England.

However, ten days into the voyage, Thomas sought a private interview with the captain. He accused his four companions of murdering the crew and afterwards sailing the *Veronica* close to the coast of South America. On 20 December, the ship was burnt on Rau's orders and the five men took to a lifeboat that was stocked with provisions, charts, a sextant and a compass. They reached Cajueira after a few days where they waited for a ship to take them to England. The cook insisted he had been forced to take part in the mutiny against his will and had killed no one.

The other four were not told of the accusations made against them and on reaching Lisbon, Captain Browne visited the British Consul, who on hearing of the cook's account, telegraphed the authorities at home. The captain was asked to sail to Liverpool where the four alleged mutineers were subsequently questioned by the police. They denied any crimes had taken place but they were arrested and charged with mutiny, arson and murder. Determined to discover the truth, the government dispatched Inspector Duckworth of the Liverpool police across the Atlantic to Ship Island where he was able to confirm the identities of the *Veronica*'s crew. It was also arranged for the pilot who escorted the *Veronica* out of the harbour to travel to England and testify at the trial. Furthermore, the crown agreed to accept Flohr's offer to turn King's Evidence and testify against the other three accused. It was realised that he had played some part in the mutiny but his involvement was thought to have been limited.

Thomas and Flohr said tensions quickly developed amongst the crew. Flohr told of seeing Schmidt being struck by McLeod very early into the voyage for failing to carry out an order and accusing him of being a poor sailor. Doran agreed with the first mate's assessment and bragged that he was a superior seaman to the foreigners on board. Rau was enraged and claimed he was a better sailor than the officers and the British crew as he had served in the German Navy and was thus able to navigate a ship. Thomas provided confirmation that strains grew between the officers and the German crewmembers and Schmidt. Like Flohr, he described being approached by Rau who said that he understood the officers were planning to throw the German crewmembers overboard. Rau produced a revolver and Schmidt also possessed one. They said they had decided to kill the officers and any of the crew who refused to join the mutiny.

The trial of Rau, Schmidt and Monson opened in Liverpool before Mr Justice Lawrance on 12 May and lasted for two days. The crown was unable to offer any motive for the crimes committed by the defendants other than the tensions that had developed among the crew in the early stages of the voyage. Given the sometimes massive differences in the accounts of the murders given by the key witnesses, it is not possible to provide a definitive account of what occurred on the *Veronica*, but some idea can be gained from the evidence given from the witness box.

Thomas and Flohr agreed that the mutiny began in the early hours of 7 December when Doran was on lookout duty and Johansen was at the wheel. Rau approached Doran and asked if he could see the North Star. This would not have seemed an unusual question as the barque was nearing the equator and sailors would be looking out for the star to aid with navigation. Doran bent down slightly as his view of the night sky was blocked by a sail. As he did so, Rau struck him violently to the head with a belaying pin. Barely conscious, Doran was carried to his cabin and possibly not realising the seriousness of the situation, he returned to the deck seeking a glass of water. Instead, Rau killed him by striking him several violent blows to the head and his lifeless body was thrown into the sea by Johansen and Flohr.

McLeod came on deck a little later and asked Rau where Paddy was. Rau made no attempt to answer and using the belaying pin, beat the first mate unconscious and it was not clear if McLeod was dead when his attacker threw him overboard. Rau and Schmidt produced their revolvers and went in search of the captain and second mate. Moments later, a number of shots were heard and Abrahamson emerged from his cabin, crying out, 'I am shot!' Captain Shaw opened his cabin door and he too was shot twice by Rau, but was able to return inside and lock himself in. Johansen was still at the wheel but on hearing the shots and screams, he started to run towards the captain's cabin, hoping to find safety. Yet, before he was able to do so, he was shot by Monson.

Thomas had been sleeping in his bunk but was wakened by the noise. Suddenly, Rau barged into the cabin brandishing a revolver and threatening to kill him. The cook begged for his life and Rau screamed, 'Ask no questions and we will spare your life.' He demanded that he make coffee for the mutineers and after doing so, Rau ordered him to drink from the pot before anyone else, lest he had poisoned the coffee or possibly added a sedative. The captain and second mate were now both in the former's cabin as Rau assumed control of the vessel. The surviving crewmembers were on deck, apparently helping him. Some were clearly doing so only because they felt intimidated and in the hope of saving their own lives.

Two days passed and Rau decided that he needed to get his hands on the charts, compass and sextant which remained in the captain's possession. Rau called out to the two officers and Captain Shaw responded by asking him, 'What have I done to be treated so? I never knew anything was wrong with the ship. Why didn't you tell me if anything was wrong? I have a wife and children. Can't you spare my life?' He pleaded for water as both he and Abrahamson were badly injured. Rau agreed to the request and provided the officers with a little food and water in exchange for the aids to navigation he required. The captain and mate remained in the cabin for a further two days, by which time they were desperate for food, water and medicines. Rau urged them to come out, promising they would come to no harm. They took him at his word but it proved to be a fatal error of judgement. Schmidt shot the second mate as he came out and wounded him in his shoulder, but Abrahamson rushed to the ship's side and jumped into the ocean. Rau walked up to the captain and shot him in the head, killing him instantly and threw his corpse overboard. Rau feared that Abrahamson may have survived and ordered a search to be made of the vicinity. He was eventually seen swimming in the water and was fired on until he disappeared beneath the waves.

Thomas insisted that Flohr attempted to shoot him but the revolver misfired twice and he was therefore able to find shelter. He had again pleaded with Rau to spare his life and Schmidt spoke up on his behalf saying Thomas had done nothing to hinder them. He remained locked in a cabin for the night and the following morning was told by Rau that his life would be spared as they believed that should he decide to betray them, he being a black man would mean that his account would never be believed.

Rau assembled the remaining members of the crew on deck and told them he and Schmidt planned to sail the *Veronica* closer to the shore where she would be burnt. They would fill a lifeboat with enough provisions to last until they reached land where they would jettison the charts and navigation aids to await rescue, which Rau knew would not take long. He had prepared a story to tell their rescuers, which was subsequently told to the captain of the *Brunswick*. Over the following days, Rau demanded that the men learn the story in detail so they would all give similar accounts and not raise any suspicions. He would stand over each man, revolver in hand, asking him to repeat the agreed version. According to Flohr, as they came closer to land and were preparing to burn the boat, it became clear that Bravo and Parsons were having difficulty in recalling the account in the necessary detail. This led to both men being shot. According to Flohr, Rau murdered Parsons and Schmidt shot Bravo. However, Thomas was adamant that it was Flohr who shot Bravo and although this was rejected by the crown, he repeated the claim in his testimony at the trial.

When first arrested, Monson claimed to have acted in self-defence, having been warned by Thomas that the officers intended to kill him and the other suspects. He acknowledged that he fought with McLeod, but that the first mate had jumped over the side when he realised he was losing the struggle. At the trial, he repeated what he had told the Liverpool police: 'We have not done anything wrong as we fought for our lives.' Schmidt also testified that he acted in self-defence as he was struck and kicked in the face by McLeod. He complained to the captain who refused to act against the mate and threatened to throw Schmidt into the sea. Schmidt also told of unrest developing because initially the food served to the seamen was of a poor quality and afterwards relationships deteriorating even further. Rau also denied responsibility for what occurred on board the *Veronica*. He witnessed what he alleged was the ill-treatment of Schmidt by the officers and was also warned by Thomas that the captain and mates were about to kill him and Schmidt. The mutiny was said to have been orchestrated by Thomas who shot Captain Shaw when he left his cabin and Flohr had murdered Abrahamson.

It was thought at one stage that a new trial would have to be arranged after a juror fell seriously ill part way through the hearing. The judge directed, however, that a new juror be sworn and the judge's notes of the earlier evidence be read to him, which took three hours. At the conclusion of the summing up, the jury retired for fifteen minutes and rejected the accounts of the defendants who had attempted to lay responsibility for the crimes on the crown's witnesses as they were all found guilty. Nonetheless, they added a strong recommendation for mercy in respect of Monson due to his youth. On 26 May, news was received from the Home Office that his sentence had been commuted to one of penal servitude for life.

Rau and Schmidt were executed alongside each other at Liverpool's Walton Prison on 2 June by hangman William Billington who was assisted by his brother John. Schmidt remained silent throughout the process and Rau's last words were: 'I am innocent of the deaths of those men.'

14

The *Durban Castle*, 1947

It was 10 October 1947 when the passenger ship *Durban Castle*, under the command of Captain Arthur Patey, left Cape Town to begin the fourteen-day voyage to Southampton. Weighing 17,382 tons and almost 600 feet in length, she was carrying fifty-seven first-class passengers. Among them was an attractive twenty-one-year-old English actress, Eileen Isabella Ronnie Gibson, who was known to her friends and family as Gay. She occupied Cabin 126 on B Deck on the port side, which was also referred to as the Shade Deck. Gay was born in India, but was raised mainly in England and took to the stage when she was seventeen years old. She had been in South Africa to appear in a play called *Golden Boy*. Despite poor reviews and its early closure, her parents would later say she was returning to Europe as she had been offered a part in a production being staged by Dublin's prestigious Abbey Theatre.

James Camb, a handsome thirty-one-year-old Lancastrian, was a steward responsible for seeing to the needs of the first-class passengers during the voyage. Although a married man, whose wife Margaret and the couple's three-year-old daughter lived in the family home in Glasgow, he was a notorious womaniser. Camb boasted of having seduced a number of women who were travelling alone in the past and he noticed Gay as soon as she came aboard, whispering to a colleague as she walked by, 'She's mine.' Within days, he was seen flirting with her and he boasted to Eileen Field, a stewardess, that he had already visited her cabin on a number of occasions. Field expressed surprise and was concerned that he was apparently involved in an intimate relationship with her and warned him against continuing to see the actress.

On the night of 18 October, with the ship cruising in shark-infested waters, there was a dance in the lounge. Gay sat at a table alone but danced with several men. She was served a number of drinks by Camb who was heard to say to her: 'I have a bone to pick with you and a big bone at that.' The band stopped playing shortly after midnight and as another steward, Bill Potts, was tidying the room he noticed Gay leaning over the ship's rail, smoking a cigarette and talking with another passenger, Frank Hopwood. A few minutes later, Potts saw Gay heading towards her cabin alone, but after a short time she appeared on deck once more where she explained to Bill Conway, the ship's maintenance man, that it was so hot in her cabin she was unable to sleep. Nevertheless, she said goodnight to Conway who watched her walk away. She was never seen again.

There were two buzzers in Cabin 126, one of which was used to summon the head steward and the other to call the deck stewardess. At a few minutes to three o'clock in the morning, both rang simultaneously. Neither the head steward nor the stewardess was on duty so it fell to stewards Jim Murray and Fred Steer to respond. On reaching Gay's cabin, Steer pushed the door open a few inches, but a man's voice called out 'It's all right' as the door was closed from within. Despite not seeing the man's face, Steer caught a glimpse of his clothes and recognised part of a steward's uniform. As both men left, he turned to Murray and said, 'That's Camb in there.' Nevertheless, the stewards felt uneasy and twenty minutes later, Murray returned to the cabin to check if all was well. Murray could see the light was on but it was quiet and believing there were no problems, he returned to his quarters. At four o'clock in the morning, Steer also decided to make sure everything was all right and returned to Gay's cabin. By this time the light was switched off and he too believed there was no need to disturb Gay and left.

At seven-thirty, Eileen Field knocked on the cabin door to rouse Gay as she had done every morning since the voyage began. Receiving no response, she pushed the door open and was surprised to find the cabin empty. Field began to make the bed and was shocked to see what she recognised to be bloodstains on the sheets. She decided to check Gay's wardrobe and as she had helped her unpack on the first day and to choose her outfits in the days that followed, Field realised that her distinctive yellow nightgown and black silk pyjamas were the only items to be missing. Field became alarmed as she knew Gay had not dressed and would not leave the cabin wearing only those garments and so rushed to the captain to advise him of her concerns.

Captain Patey arranged for a thorough search of the ship to be made but there was no trace of the missing actress, nor did she respond to a request to report to a member of the crew given over the ship's public address system. The captain gave the order for the ship to turn around so that a search of the ocean might be made but this proved to be fruitless. A more thorough search was made of the cabin and yellow and black fibres were discovered on the rim of the open porthole. The captain knew she must have jumped through it to commit suicide or was pushed through the porthole dead or alive. He questioned the members of the crew who had spoken to her at the dance and also to the passenger Frank Hopwood. They all described her as being in good spirits, which suggested suicide was unlikely.

Captain Patey was convinced a murder had been committed and suspected that Camb was involved in her disappearance. Camb, however, insisted he had not been in Gay's cabin following the dance and that he knew nothing of the previous night's events. The captain remained suspicious and asked Anthony Griffiths, the ship's doctor, to examine the steward and a number of scratches were discovered on his body. Older marks were found on his left collarbone and there were more recent ones on the back of his right shoulder and on his right wrist. Camb denied they were inflicted while making love to Gay or in a struggle with her as she resisted his advances and explained that they were self-inflicted. The older marks were caused by having a severe itch on a very hot night and the more recent ones had appeared a few hours earlier as he dried himself too vigorously with a towel. Far from satisfied with Camb's story, Captain Patey telegraphed his employers in England, giving details of the young woman's disappearance and his suspicions regarding the steward's possible responsibility. When the ship docked in Southampton on 24 October, Detective Sergeant John Quinlan of the local police force was waiting.

Camb had by this time come to recognise that the account he gave to the captain lacked credibility and when interviewed by Sergeant Quinlan, he admitted to having sexual liaisons with passengers in the past and also with Gay. Camb said he visited her on the night of her disappearance by arrangement and as soon as he entered the cabin, she took off her nightgown, beneath which she was naked. As they were making love, she suddenly clutched him and dug her fingernails into his flesh. She was struggling for breath and after a few moments her body went limp. Camb attempted to resuscitate her but she soon died and he pushed both buzzers simultaneously to summon assistance. However, as he waited for help to arrive, it dawned on him that he would lose his job for having a sexual relationship with a passenger and he would be unable to support his family. In a state of panic, he decided to push her through the porthole and hope his involvement would not become known. There was a knock on the door when the stewards arrived and he shouted out 'It's all right.' The porthole was directly above the bed and with much difficulty Camb was able to accomplish the task and heard her body hit the water with a loud splash. He insisted she was dead and that his actions were not intended to cover up her murder, but simply to save his job and to prevent his wife finding out he was an adulterer.

Camb's second account was also disbelieved and despite the absence of a corpse, the crown was convinced there was enough circumstantial evidence to arrest and charge him with Gay's murder. His trial was delayed for several weeks as the defence lawyers arranged for three witnesses to make the journey from South Africa. They were Henry Gilbert, the producer of *Golden Boy*, his wife, Dr Ina Schaub, and actor Mike Abel. The trial eventually opened at Winchester Assizes on 18 March 1948 and lasted for four days.

The crown claimed that on the night of the murder, the accused had not been invited to Gay's cabin for consensual sex. It was argued that Camb called on her uninvited and when she opened the door but refused to admit him, he forced his way in. The jury was asked to consider whether, if as he claimed, she had agreed to have sex with him, why was she still wearing her pyjamas and nightgown? The evidence demonstrated she must have been wearing such clothing when she was pushed through the porthole, as indicated by the discovery of fibres on its rim. Such a scenario was unlikely and it was argued Gay resisted Camb's advances as he attempted to rape her and in a rage, he strangled her. Evidence to support this was provided by pathologist Dr Donald Teare who had discovered urine on the sheets, which he stated often passed from the victims of strangulation. As she struggled, Gay scratched her attacker, thus causing the incriminating marks on Camb's body. She also managed to push both buzzers, but by the time the stewards arrived she was dead. Gay's mother, Eileen, described her daughter as a healthy and moral young woman who drank rarely. This was refuted by the defence who called evidence that portrayed her in a different light and in so doing put the alleged victim's reputation on trial.

Camb's lawyers argued that Gay's hands were not large enough to have enabled her to press both buzzers at the same time. It was not Gay who was attempting to call for help but their client who had done so to summon assistance when he became aware that she was seriously ill as they had sex. Nonetheless, in the few minutes it took for the stewards to arrive, he decided to push her through the porthole for the reasons given in his statement to Sergeant Quinlan. Doubt was also cast on the crown's claim that the scratches on Camb's body were inflicted by Gay as she attempted to fight him off. Under fierce cross-examination, Dr Griffiths conceded that he could not discount the possibility that they were caused by Gay when digging her fingers into Camb during a seizure as the couple made love. The defence hoped that major doubts had been cast on an important part of the crown's case.

The witnesses who travelled from South Africa gave compelling testimonies in support of Camb's case. Mike Abel confirmed he had a brief but intense intimate relationship with Gay and described an incident that occurred when they were making love in his car. Gay demanded that Abel say that he was in love with her and when told not to be silly as he was a married man, she suffered a seizure similar to that described by Camb. She had stopped breathing but to Abel's relief, she regained consciousness. He had also seen Gay pass out at parties, sometimes because she was drunk, but at other times she fainted when she seemed to become excited for some reason.

Henry Gilbert gave details of four sexual relationships Gay had during her stay in South Africa that he knew of. The producer's wife, Dr Schaub, told the court she was consulted by Gay who sought advice on contraception. The doctor also spoke of Gay's partying, which led her to warn the actress of the possible consequences such a hedonistic lifestyle could have on her, especially as she suffered from seizures. The defence team was clearly attempting to portray the dead woman as a heavy drinking and sexually promiscuous individual who suffered from serious health problems, which served to demonstrate that Camb's version of events was true.

The jury took forty-five minutes to convict Camb of murder and he was sentenced to death by the judge, Sir Malcolm Hilbery. His execution was provisionally set for 13 April, but was postponed as he made an unsuccessful appeal against his conviction. A petition was arranged by Mr A. P. G. Elson, a Southampton businessman, which was well supported throughout the country, but it was not this that saved his life. Late on the night of 14 April, the House of Commons voted in favour of suspending the death penalty for a trial period of five years as part of the Criminal Justice Bill that was passing through Parliament. This led the Home Secretary to reprieve Camb in the interests of natural justice who was instead sentenced to life imprisonment. This clause, however, was subsequently rejected by the Lords and executions continued. Camb was released after serving eleven years behind bars and now divorced, he returned to Lancashire. Eight years after his release, he was convicted of an indecent act with a young girl but kept his liberty. In the early Seventies, Camb appeared in court for indecent assaults on three girls and was returned to prison for several years. Following his release and divorced for a second time, he found work as a barman and died in 1979.

It would be a pity if the *Durban Castle* was remembered solely for the infamous porthole murder. She originally entered service in 1938 and during the Second World War acted as a landing ship for the invasion of North Africa, becoming the first vessel to be fired upon by the enemy in Arzeu Bay. Later, she was used in the assaults on Sicily and the south of France. In 1962, this fine ship was broken up for scrap.

Index